The Way in
Divine Metaphysics

The Way in
Divine Metaphysics

agnoi - J.D. Tarran

Order this book online at www.trafford.com
or email orders@trafford.com

Most Trafford titles are also available at major online book retailers.

Printed in the United States of America.

ISBN: 978-1-4269-9261-2 (sc)
ISBN: 978-1-4269-9260-5 (hc)
ISBN: 978-1-4269-9262-9(e)

Library of Congress Control Number: 2011960623

Trafford rev. 01/10/2011

www.trafford.com

North America & international
toll-free: 1 888 232 4444 (USA & Canada)
phone: 250 383 6864 ♦ fax: 812 355 4082

THE WAY IN DIVINE METAPHYSICS— CONTENTS

To my beloved, who inspired me,
and to all those of the Way.

With Love to my Son Laib and Daughter Wanan

The Way: Introduction

In MANY RELIGIONS, philosophies, and disciplines of spiritual growth, 'A Way' is spoken of with quiet reverence. It is, primarily a path, a discipline, and a code of conduct. The purveyors of such a path or discipline do not intend it as an artificial way devised by humankind according to the culture of a specific time and place, but frame it around an awareness of ultimate reality—of 'the Way things are.'

The Way is revealed though the divine order and accessed by mystics and contemplatives who have studied the divine order or experienced enlightenment or divine inspiration. To understand and describe the Way things are in universal terms is the goal of metaphysics, and such meaning and purpose that this brings to human life expresses an ideal Way for human individuals to follow.

This current work is a study of the many human expressions of the Way. It is not a study of the many purported truths of humankind and the many ways based on these. It is my aim to reveal that there is a Way, a Divine and Natural Way, which runs and has run as a common thread through the thinking of many peoples in the world at different times in history. This Way is subject to a developing understanding and has passed though different phases of human awareness. There can only be one truth about the existence of beings in the world, though it finds different expression in different cultures and languages. Only one Ultimate and Divine Truth can exist, for if not, there would be nothing worthy of the name 'Truth'.

This metaphysical standpoint underlies this study. Metaphysics is the area of philosophy that is concerned with what is ultimately real and true—that which is always and everywhere real and true, not simply case-specific knowledge. Any claim to universal truth is a metaphysical claim, and all competing claims to universal truth from religion, philosophy, and science can be viewed side by side and examined in the field of metaphysics.

Any Christian would say, 'Christ is the Way', and he or she may indeed be right. But Christ, as Logos and mind of God, should have had access to all wisdom, human and divine, and stood at a pinnacle of growth in divine awareness. To say or imply that Jesus would have been unaware of the wisdom of Taoism, for example, is to deny that he participated in God's greater eternal and omniscient awareness. All world religions and philosophical traditions leading up to his advent may be seen as forming the true Old Testament to this world saviour. This is the context of the current study, which deals with many of the world's most significant religious and philosophical wisdom traditions leading up to Christ and beyond.

I have been selective in the material presented, to point out recurring themes and focus on the golden thread that is the Way. However, I have also tried to highlight differences that are often important and should not be glossed over. This is a very concise introduction to the world's pearls of wisdom, and I hope it will inspire others to conduct further research and, more importantly, to attain greater and more universal awareness.

The name *metaphysics* derives from a section of the works of the great philosopher Aristotle. In these works, which concern universals and first principles, Aristotle speaks of a 'divine science', a science of the mind of God—'Being such a science that God alone could have or God before all others.'(Aristotle The Metaphysics) The 'mind of God' or 'Logos' concept in the history of ideas is one theme of this work. For seen in these terms, it is the Logos that regulates and determines the Way.

This work is a study in worldwide metaphysics. It presents and introduces all the world's most significant wisdom traditions and religious philosophies. In the book's later section, I will introduce my own metaphysical philosophy of *Equipoise*, which can then be seen against the backdrop of its inheritance in the greatest traditions of metaphysics. This metaphysical philosophy of *Equipoise* is a universal law of necessary equivalence and symmetry, involving necessary counterbalance. I hope this will serve as an indication of what metaphysics might become as a 'divine science' in taking on the crucial insights of science and the profundity of religion.

The spiritual influences that have shaped nations and influenced history through the ages are a theme of this book.

The Way in Divine Metaphysics examines one evolving truth and one Way, discovered, and not invented, through various approaches, in different environments, as seen from different perspectives.

*   *   *

Grounds of all being

Orderer of nature

Divine source

If it be thy will

So guide our Way

Love uniting all

Opposites conjoined

Very God, I pray

Every being within you, give you praise.

—agnoi 'God is Love Prayer'; the first letter of each line spell this

About the Author

About myself—agnoi (J.D.Tarran) I am the son of a Methodist and Uniting Church minister. I abandoned religion in youth and began studying science. However, after a peak mystical experience, I decided to look into the truth of all religions, and in my search, I ended up with a degree in Comparative Religious Studies and Anthropology from Australian National University. I also studied occult science at this time. I lived in the Kimberley area of Western Australia for fifteen years, where I worked as an anthropologist. There I was for a time a variety of freethinking neo-shaman learning from local Aboriginal shaman. My two children from my former marriage are Aboriginal.

In the transition of the millennia, I found myself locked in a running spiritual battle against evil, and I ended up a committed Christian, though I am still freethinking.

I fell on my feet in the Telstra divine metaphysics chat room (founded by meta) where I decided metaphysics—the only way to examine competing claims to truth and escape truth-relativism—was what I was all about, and I pursued active full-time research. My spiritual name, agnoi, was given me in spirit by the Lord Jesus. This book began in 2001 with the support of friends from the former Telstra Divine Metaphysics chat room and my now defunct web group 'The Way Divine Metaphysics'. These days, you can find me on Twitter under my spiritual name, agnoi.

Chapter 1

THE WAY OF NATURE

'Hold on to the Tao (Way) of old in order to master the things of the present.
From this one may know the primeval beginning of the universe'
(Lao tzu, *Tao Te Ching*, verse 14)

THE CHINESE WRITTEN language is very ancient, the earliest discovered forms being the pictogram inscriptions on 'dragon bones'. These are legendarily the bones of actual dragons, but unearthed as archaeological artefacts. They were inscribed with a subject and heated on a fire, and the cracks appearing in them were interpreted as oracles of the future. In Chinese culture, the dragon is considered a powerful spirit of nature involved in thunderstorms. The spiritual energy of the dragon runs through the earth in '*dragon lines*' in *feng shui* geomancy. Unlike in Western mythology, the dragon is not considered evil, but a primal power, which can bring good fortune if properly dealt with.

Prediction of the future was also a concern of one of the oldest Chinese classic books, the *I Ching* (*Book of Changes*), which uses a system of broken and unbroken lines, at some stage equated with yin and yang, in a binary system to describe all changes and events through analogy. The system is similar to the binary language used in computing, obtained from 0 and 1 alternatives and combinations. The broken (__ __) and unbroken (___) lines correctly symbolise the open and closed logic circuits involved. It is a form of proto-Taoist thought, which predates Lao Tzu and was later elaborated on by Taoist and Confucian commentators.

From ancient China comes one of the most enduring and well-known expressions of the Way—the Tao or 'Way of Nature' principally associated with the Taoist school. Simply expressed, Taoist philosophy rests in the perception that we exist in unity with nature and the ultimate reality is this underlying unity.

Using too many artificial words and concepts draws us away from awareness of this underlying unity. Concepts sever and split the unity of existence into parcels, and when this is done, the ultimate truth of unity stands in danger of being lost to our awareness. Within the unity of nature, there is an implied division into two opposites, which is purely natural. Yet even these have a secondary reality to the all-encompassing truth of their Unity.

In nature, there are light and dark, hot and cold, active and passive, above and below; and in beings, male and female. These were viewed as complementary opposites. The 'yang' and the 'yin'. Yang is light, summer, activity, force, heaven, masculinity. Yin is darkness, winter, passivity, form, earth, femininity. From their union, symbolically portrayed in the familiar Tai chi diagram ('Great ultimate'—yin and yang) all existence results. These two opposites interact dynamically in cycles, creating all things, as well as leading to their passing away.

The Way of Nature—Tao—being the ultimate truth implied an ideal path for humanity. Taoism suggests that we must follow a path of balance, practice meditative stillness of mind in order to keep the truth of unity foremost, and not let the mind become cluttered and confused. Lao Tzu's great work, the *Tao Te Ching*, which founded the Taoist school, also states that this is the Way of rulers, whether they be socially recognized emperors or the unknown rulers, the hermit sages. The latter, by being identified with Tao, the organising principle of Nature, influenced events though 'non-action' (*wui we*) and without claiming responsibility for them.

The founder of Taoism was Lao Tzu, who lived in the sixth century BC, though his single text, the *Tao Te Ching*, may have been worked over by other Taoists.

His ideal state of being was in unity with the all, like a block undifferentiated from a tree, cleansed and pure of mind like a child. He wrote, 'Who by unending discipline of the senses embraces unity, cannot be disintegrated. By concentrating his vitality and inducing tenderness he can become like a little child. By purifying, cleansing, and profound intuition he can be free from faults' (*Tao Te Ching*, verse 10).

What Lao Tzu means by the Tao (Way) is mysteriously profound, beyond logical conception but indicates the origin and implicit order of all. 'Hold on to the Tao (Way) of old in order to master the things of the present. From this one may know the primeval beginning of the universe' (*Tao Te Ching*, verse 14)

Lao Tzu seemed to anticipate Christ when he wrote, 'He who loves the world as his body may be entrusted with the empire' (*Tao Te Ching*, verse 13).

Another verse which might indicate or prophecy Christ is the following- 'He who suffers disgrace for his country, Is called Lord of the Land. He who takes upon himself the country's misfortunes, becomes King of the Empire' (*Tao Te Ching*, verse 78).

Lao Tzu saw heaven as the ruling power of earth, which ruled through love. He wrote, 'For deep love helps one to win in the case of attack, and be firm in the case of defence. When heaven is to save a person, Heaven will protect them through deep love' (*Tao Te Ching*, verse 67).

It should be mentioned, however, that the concept of Love as a unifying principle uniting opposites (my own concept), which relates to Tao, is not found explicitly in Taoism. In fact, there are various translations of the *Tao Te Ching* in which the word *love* (*jen*, 'humanity' or 'love') do not occur. Though Love as principle uniting opposites may be considered implicit in the yin-yang theory of Taoism.

Taoism provides the basis of many mind-body systems of development and martial arts training, including tai chi, tai bo, taikwondo, qigong, and kung fu.

In China, Taoism was to partly blend with Buddhism imported from India. This was the 'middle way' of the Buddha, who emphasized compassion, detachment, and expanded awareness. However, it might have just as readily been syncretized with Christianity. An early Jesuit translation of the *Tao Te*

Ching rendered the word *Tao* as *God*. A more modern translation by Paul Carus translates *Tao* as *reason*, though making it clear in the introduction that *reason* refers to the divine reason or the Logos. Its most usual translation, however, is *Way*. All translations appearing in this chapter come from the invaluable sourcebook of Professor Wing-tsit Chan, which retranslates all the classic works of Chinese philosophy.

Confucius, who was roughly the contemporary of Lao Tzu and may have travelled to meet him (later to liken him to a dragon), also speaks of the Way or the Tao. A classical debate between Confucianists and Taoists ran through the millennia of Chinese history, as to the value of the social status and hierarchy that Confucius upheld whilst Taoists were egalitarian. Confucius and Lao Tzu yet found common ground.

'Confucius said, In the Morning hear the Way, in the evening die content' (*Analects* 4:8).
Confucius related the concept of Tao, the Way, to virtue, which was learnt through wisdom. 'Unless there is perfect virtue the perfect Way cannot be materialised' (*The Mean*, chapter 27).

The *Doctrine of the Mean* (sometimes translated as *Chung Yung*, meaning not bent in any direction and unswerving, the central in the universal) advances a related concept of a balanced good that is natural and inborn. This concept owed something to both Lao Tzu and Mencius, whose teaching, 'jen is *jen*' or 'humanity is human nature', referred to original human goodness at birth.

'What heaven (*T'ien*) imparts to a man is called human nature. To follow our nature is called the Way ...

'Equilibrium is the great foundation of the world, and harmony is the universal path' (Confucius, *Doctrine of the Mean*, verse 1).

Chuang Tzu followed both Lao Tzu and Confucius, elaborating the Way of Nature, 'Tao', in a more distinctly metaphysical treatment. 'Although the universe is vast, its transformation is uniform. Although the myriad things are many, their order is one' (Chuang Tzu, *Tao as Transformation and One*, chapter 5.)

The order of all things and the means through which they come into being is 'Tao', the Way, which creatively unifies all things, the origin of all the principle-patterns inherent in nature.

According to Chuang Tzu, 'When "this" and "that" have no opposites, there is the very axis of Tao. Only when the axis occupies the very centre of a circle can things in their infinite complexity be responded to' (*The Equality of Things*, chapter 2).

The Legalists picked up the concept of Tao (the Way) and related it to law, following from natural law. The principal legalist philosopher, Han Fei Tzu, was influential in the Chin Dynasty unification where the unified 'China' takes its name in 221 BC. The regime opposed Confucian feudal orthodoxy and actively swept away old culture and learning, burning books except for practical works and notable classics such as the *I Ching*. An age later (2,179 years) and this was to happen again under the Communist Cultural Revolution, which saw books burnt and academics sent to practical farm work.

Han Fei Tzu presented an interesting discussion of Tao, which represents something of a development, as it emphasizes the Way as the basic ordering principle from which all true principles derive.

'Tao (The Way) is that by which all things become what they are. It is that with which all principles are commensurable. Principles are patterns (*wen*) according to which things come into being, and Tao is the cause of their being. Therefore it is said that Tao (The Way) puts things in order (*li*)" (Han Fei Tzu verse 2, *Interpretations of Tao*).

Both these meanings are implied in the original Taoist concept of Tao, the Way, which was at once the unity of all and the principle unifying all. In nature this is expressed as natural law, and following from this, we find the ideal that regulates human nature, law, and social order.

The ancient Chinese concept of a lord of heaven (Shang-Ti) from the Shang Dynasty (dragon lord emperors) had increasingly fallen out of use by the time of the sages Lao Tzu and Confucius and was replaced by an impersonal will of heaven (*T'ien*) or the principle regulating the interaction of heaven and earth (Tao). However it is quite possible to form a view of Tao in which consciousness is implicit, as it is in Logos, seen as the ordering intelligence of God, which has ordered all nature in its creation.

Chapter 2

THE WAY OF THE SHAMAN

'All are really One.'
—Black Elk

In most, if not all human societies, there has existed a type of person highly attuned to spiritual realities, who commonly uses his or her gifts to heal others and to regulate events in society. Anthropologists use the name *shaman* (originally Siberian, from the Vedic *sram*, to ignite) to describe such a practitioner and spiritual healer of whatever culture and society, which might be Australian Aboriginal, North or South American Indian, Inuit, Polynesian, African, Asian, and so on. More recently, this type of understanding has been applied to the study of traditional practitioners of Europeans societies, such as the Celts and their Druids.

In talking of Shamanism, we are not talking of a coherent worldwide religion or belief system, for a diversity of beliefs are found in formerly non-communicating cultures. Yet there are many common elements among the varieties of Shamanism, and the Way of the Shaman is best seen as a purely natural human capacity or practice, revealing itself in different forms in different societies.

Many Christians shy away from the implication of pagan magical practices. Yet in the broad definition of shamanism, the Lord Jesus himself was a divine shaman, who accomplished feats of healing by dealing with spirits and the spiritual realm as the cause of disease, madness, and social problems.

A Priest relates humankind to God; a Shaman relates God to humankind. A Shaman deals immediately with spiritual reality and only secondarily with the social world. However, in particular societies, a universal spirit and a variety of animal spirits and hybrid spiritual beings may be more common expressions of the shamans' spiritual realm, which is one of unity with all nature.

What can be seen to characterize shamanism as a worldwide phenomenon is an initiatory crises often in solitude in nature (the Christian parallel is Christ in the wilderness), where the person feeling the calling is immersed in a purely spiritual and not social reality.

This may involve a kind of symbolic death and rebirth to a new life in greater spiritual awareness. The ability to deal with both helping spirits (allies) and spiritual adversaries is acquired. The shaman may acquire the ability to travel in spirit alone, commonly visiting both the sky realm and the earth realm in his or her travels. Communication at a distance and the ability to control the forces of nature—in other words, rainclouds, thunderstorms, wind, waves, and so on—are possible shamanic gifts.

Mediating between sky realm and earth realm and between the spiritual and human social worlds, shamans may use chanting, percussion, or other means, including natural drugs, to enter the plane of spiritual reality, though these outer techniques, like trickery and ritual trappings, are not essential.

What characterizes shamanism in particular is not so much an inherited tradition of any sort but the freethinking ability to organize and make sense of such paranormal experiences, which the layperson would think of as madness. The shaman is a practitioner of 'crazy wisdom'—deep insight that lends itself to expressions that resolve particular tensions in the spiritual realm, though uncommon and original expressions, often with characteristic humour.

The Way of the Shaman is also a path of balance. When confronted by threatening spiritual influences, two opposite imbalanced responses are fear and anger. The shaman learns to minimize these and deal with a clear head and an intuitive response to spiritual dangers.

When a shaman sees a person suffering sickness, they may see a person badly affected by spiritual invasion, which has left the sufferer's bodily system weak and perhaps his or her child spirit absent. When they see a person talking crazily or in a fit of anger, they see spiritual invasion. The expression 'What got into you?' is a spiritual reality for a shaman. When they see a criminal punished, a shaman may see the real culprit, a spirit influence, escaping. Only a shaman can deal with these situations. A shaman comes to see social events as having underlying spiritual shaping causes, and commonly enforce their own version of divine law. They may escort spirits to places of confinement or reconcile them.

But a shaman also has a vision of the divine order obtained through direct experience and may lead others into it, whether through communication by language or simply by the spiritual potency of his or her reordering of sky realm and earth realm, or heaven and earth.

Common techniques include *spirit flight*, travelling in the spirit body; *spirit capture*, restoring a sick, dying, or dead person's wandering child spirit or soul or dealing with troublesome spirits; *dream work*, remaining conscious in dreaming to obtain visions and to affect dreaming outcomes that might affect future events; and *ritual use of intent*, holding a firm intent to effect change through a flawless ritual. *Divination* and *psychosomatic healing techniques* are also common practices. The molten core of the earth was known to shamans through spirit travel before it was known to science. Only pure or purified spirits may pass through.

Many shamans, including those here in North West Australia, believed crystals to be effective in trapping and directing spiritual energy. Sceptics of 'crystal magic' would do well to bear in mind that science continues to discover new properties of crystals (prismatic, piezoelectric, semi-conductive, and the like).

The chants of shaman, while they can contribute to a shift in consciousness, are often believed to have associated magical effects, a 'singing into being'. A similar tradition of belief is found in the Druid and Bard traditions in Celtic culture, where the songs of the bards might evoke different atmospheres and effects. The mantras of Buddhists or prayer chants in other religions are related phenomena.

Australian Aboriginal religion, like many others, is built up from the traditions passed on by its shaman innovators. What is unique and characteristic about it is its belief in 'the Eternal Dreaming' (*Buggarigarra* here in North West Australia) It is a concept moving toward a unity of beings in eternity, so that ancient themes and encounters have continued relevance in the present day. In this realm, the spirits of ancestral beings—such as the ancient giant serpents (whose bones have been discovered) and legendary shaman innovators who were culture heroes—and their activities retain eternal reality. The dreaming may be entered in inspired dreams or in altered states, sometimes accompanied by ritual. In this religion, song records the passage of ancestral beings through the landscape in dreaming trails, also known as 'songlines'.

Song can be a means of developing and using an 'inner voice'. If you have ever had a catchy song running through your mind, you will be aware that it is possible to 'sing' without vocalising aloud. Rather, you hear the song with your inner hearing. This can lead to gifts such as telepathic sending and spirit travel, through becoming aware of the source and location of your 'spirit voice' and formation of 'spirit choruses'. Short repetitive chants are the most effective.

I believe that the power of songs and music is very often underestimated in our society. Whether or not it is true that songs or chants can influence objective reality, they most certainly influence subjective perceptions of it. A person habitually singing along to depressive or darkly frightening lyrics should beware of negative consequences in his or her life.

However, there are possibilities of effects that go beyond the subjective. Like many others around the world, I sang along to the "Free Nelson Mandela" song while Mandela was imprisoned. I believe those who did so contributed to enabling the post-apartheid South Africa that he led as president.

A lesson that might be taken more broadly from the shamanic singing into being tradition of belief or the Australian aboriginal tradition of singing certain people to their death (often a law-based punishment) is to sing positively, not for what you do not wish to happen.

Purity, which in a shamanic context meant freedom from harmful spirits and their influence, was believed to be obtained through a number of means in different cultures.

Water cleansings could be effective, although I have also read of saltwater immersion depriving a shaman of his helpful 'doctor spirits'. Smoking ceremonies are often used to clear out spirits, and in North West Australia, *goongara* wood is used for this. *Goongara* is a variety of sandalwood and similar to incense, which is also sandalwood-based, used in Asian traditions and in some Christian churches. Sweat lodges, a type of sauna bath, were used by North American Indian shaman. In some ancient cultures, including Japan, the sprinkling of salt is believed to spiritually purify.

It is important to distinguish shamanism from the related phenomena of 'spiritualism'. This tradition grew up in Europe out of a desire to prove the reality of spirit to the sceptical and scientific minds of the time. It was essentially a performance and often concerned with contacting spirits of the dead using mediums. A shaman does not characteristically summon spirits for information but works with such spirits as are around for a healing purpose. I believe seekers of truth should be wary of accepting information from spirits; such information is often distorted by confluences (spiritual admixtures).

I have presented the Way of the Shaman as a kind of belief system without critique, though shamanic beliefs differ widely. But there is, in the recurring of common themes of belief in different, formerly non-communicating cultures of the world, the basis of an argument based on verification. If one person perceives something no one else can perceive, he or she might be dismissed as suffering illusion. But if many perceive it, that something may be regarded as verified. From extension of this principle, one would have to ask why so many independent peoples of the world could regard both the existence of spirits and the abilities of workers with spirits as genuine if there were no foundation to this belief. But another relevant question asks for an explanation of the extent of disagreement among these belief systems.

Mind, culture, and different language concepts appear to affect impressions of the spiritual realm, and this is part of the answer. The ability of spirits to mix and form unique hybrids through confluence—in other words, of man and animal—is another, which may vary according to the natural environment. A North American shaman may have dealings with an otter-woman or an Australian shaman with an emu-man.

I venture that, rather than being a kind of insubstantial substance with wispy existence, spirit is concerned with the ultimate reality of unity in eternity, appearing in the temporal and transient 'reality'. A being which exists physically in a discrete duration, then, maintains a kind of existence enduringly within eternal unity. However, as spirits move toward the unitary and united reality, they are involved in confluence, or mixing, over time and space. The effects of this may be either deleterious or beneficial to a human.

Spirit is the intermediate between the ultimate reality of unity in eternity, inclusive of all time and space, and the temporal reality of the present. Spirit transcends time and space; it is the impression of the eternal unity of all in the transient and overrides transient separateness.

Shamanism can be seen as a type of applied metaphysics and a tradition of adventurous experimentation in dealing with spiritual phenomenon.

Chapter 3

THE WAY OF THE BRAHMIN

'Repeating OM, the one syllable, Brahma, and thinking on me, when he goes forth abandoning a body, he goes the highest Way'(Bhagavad Gita 8:15).

BUDDHISM HAD ITS origins in India, against the older backdrop of Hinduism. Hinduism upheld a strict caste system, in which the upper caste was the Brahmin caste, the Hereditary priesthood. Souls could, in theory, achieve more favourable reincarnations in higher castes through the merit of their former lives and the karma they accrued.

Hinduism can take a whole variety of local forms and recognizes a whole plethora of gods, two of the major ones being Vishnu the preserver and Shiva the destroyer. Others include Indra, Rama, Krishna, and Agni the fire-being. However, the penultimate expression of Hinduism in the Upanishads is that all gods are one God in Brahman (or Brahma, gender neutral), the Universal being, who is one with the *atman*, the innermost self within. This realization was what successive reincarnations led up to, before liberation from the cycle of rebirth was possible. The Upanishads are the most mystical and metaphysical section of the Hindu scriptures. The word *Upanishad* means 'sit down near' and carries the sense of the secret teaching transmitted from master to pupil.

The Way of the Hindu Brahmin involves seeking the *atman*, the inner self. 'He who abiding in the understanding is other than the understanding, whom the understanding does not know, whose body is the understanding, who controls the understanding from within: He is the self within you, the inner controller, the immortal' (Brihadaranyaka Upanishad 3:7:22).

Through the practice of yoga (literally, yoking, uniting, or integration), greater awareness was obtained. This included *siddhis*, psychic gifts and paranormal abilities and, eventually, the experience of enlightenment.

In full awareness, to be one with the universal being, Brahma, often through the personal Lord *Ishvara* was the goal of yoga, and the Way of the Brahmin. Yoga can take a number of forms—*dyana yoga* (meditational); *karma yoga* (ritual devotion); *bhakti yoga* (relationship with godhead based on human relationship analogies of lover, father, teacher, friend, and so on); *hatha yoga* (physical mind-body), *tantric yoga* (divine union, sexual); and *kundalini yoga* (awakening primal energy).

In the Bhagavad Gita, a 'Way' is spoken of as ultimate unity with the supreme being. 'But beyond that there is another being, unmanifested, eternal, beyond the manifested, which when all things perish, perishes not. The unmanifested, the indestructible it is called; they call it the supreme Way. When they have obtained it they return not. This is my supreme abode' (Bhagavad Gita 8:20).

The objects of perception are described in terms of *maya* (illusion or lesser transient reality). The Upanishads indicate that, through realizing the ultimate reality of being one with Brahman (God), one may see through the illusion of transient appearance—*maya*.'By becoming what one really is the whole world of appearance (*maya*) will be lost to sight at last' (Svetasvatra Upanishad 1:10).

But also, Brahman, the universal being, is at times identified in a pantheistic way with all that exists. "All this is Brahman" (Chandogya Upanishad III; 14; 1).

This leaves an issue when it comes to what is real and of Brahman and what is transient or illusory.

Sankara and Ramanuja are 'Vedanta' philosophers. In other words, their philosophy is built from the Upanishads, which are the 'end of the Vedas', Hindu sacred scriptures. A principal theme of the Upanishads is the identity of atman and Brahman (or Brahma—gender neutral). This involves the inner self, atman, and the identity of this self of all with the universal being,

Brahma (God), further identified as the impersonal absolute or ultimate reality.

The two forms of knowing required to realise the unity of the inner self and the universal being are identified in the Svetasvtara Upanishad as *Sankhya* (philosophy) and yoga (integration meditation).

The various writers of the Upanishads had a common tradition but different manners of conceptualising this profound area of Hindu thought. Their treatment was more poetic than resembling systematic reasoned philosophy. So it was that there was room for further refinement and exposition of this metaphysical core of Hinduism.

Sankara of the ninth century AD and Ramanuja of the eleventh century AD were the two most influential Hindu philosophers and metaphysicians.

Sankara (or Shankara) was of the Brahmin caste, a priest who did not pass through a period of life as a married householder, contrary to the tradition, and passed the practice of celibacy on to his followers in communities called *mathas* that he established. He defined the goal of his philosophy as the discovery of that which, when known, makes all known. He emphasised the distinction from the Mundaka Upanishad between *para vidya*, higher knowledge, and *apara vidya*, lower knowledge. In Sankara's terms, *para vidya* did not involve the *upadis*, the limiting conditions of the intellect, but knew through direct intuition without the interaction of subject and object. Sankara took up a position against the illusion of the empirical world, *maya*, and the unreality of name and form imposed on the world by *avidya*, false knowledge.

He drew an analogy depicting a man with defective vision who may see more than one moon, though there is only one. Similarly, through false knowledge, *avidya*, we see multiplicity in what is, in reality, only the unity of Brahma (God).

Sankara's philosophy is called Advaita. It is a philosophy of 'non-dualism,' for Sankara recognised only the ultimate unitary reality of Brahma as real, while the phenomenal world *maya* was neither real nor unreal in his exposition.

Ramanuja's philosophy is called 'Vishishtadvaita.' In contrast to Advaita, it is a philosophy of qualified non-dualism. Ramanuja accorded reality to matter and to individual souls as proceeding from and dependant on Brahman. He argued against the 'illusion' interpretation of *maya* by asking, if so, where does the illusion proceed from? It cannot be from God, since he does not make errors, and it cannot be from the individual, since individuals are only the product of the illusion according to Advaita non-dualism.

Ramanuja placed more stress on the distinction between the eternal and transient realities, speaking of *maya* as the realm of the transient changeable things, which were nonetheless real in their material form, contingent on the one eternal God.

'This great unborn self, undecaying, undying immortal, fearless, is indeed Brahman. Fearless is the Brahman, and he who knows this becomes verily the fearless Brahman' (Katha Upanishad 3:1).

Passages like this one prompt a question: If there is a universal being indwelling in all beings, to what degree is it justifiable to identify with this universal God ? The enlightenment of the Hindu Brahmins equated self with God. A logical problem this entails is that, if the inner self or atman of all human beings Is Brahma (God) then the inner self of all beings is the same self; in other words, there is no true individual selfhood. Why then should humans disagree?

* * *

The Buddha Siddhartha Gautama (sixth century BC) reacted so strongly to this paradox (and the seemingly egotistic expression of 'I am God') that he rejected both the selfhood of the individual and of the greater universal awareness. He rejected the search for the atman (the inner self) as a mistaken quest.

For the Buddha, the true Brahmin did not become so by birth or caste. 'A man becomes not a Brahmin by long hair or family or birth. The man in whom there is truth and holiness, he is in joy and he is a Brahmin" (*Dhammapada* 393).

The Buddha democratised the seeking of the Way.

'He whose vision is deep, who is wise, who knows the Way, and what is outside the Way, who has attained the highest end—him I call a Brahmin' (*Dhammapada* 403).

The Buddha's 'Middle Way' was, firstly, a path between extremes of indulgence in worldly pleasures and of rigorous asceticism and self-mortification. To some degree, it also implied balance in other areas; for example, it urged regarding both praise and blame with equal detachment.

After contemplating long on the causes of suffering, the historical Buddha Siddhartha Gautama reached enlightenment and announced the 'four noble truths'.

Since all things and all beings are transient in the sensible world, suffering is consequent both in their birth and coming into being and in their inevitable loss. This is the first noble truth.

Loss would not cause suffering but for craving for existence. This is the second noble truth.

This craving for existence depends on the illusion of selfhood and can be eliminated. This is the third noble truth.

The manner in which illusion, craving, and suffering are overcome is the middle Way and involves the noble eightfold path—right views, right aspirations, right speech, right behaviour, right livelihood, right effort, right thoughts, and right contemplation. This is the fourth noble truth.

Buddhism does not generally concern itself with talk of 'God', for the ultimate reality, the *Dharma kaya*, which is beyond all predicates, is not generally conceived as a being with selfhood. Still, it is the origin of dharma (sacred law). The Buddhist goal was liberation from illusion, desire, egocentrism, and rebirth. The *nama rupa*, realm of names and forms, was considered a source of illusion.

However, liberating a self that does not exist as an abiding soul from reincarnation it cannot truly undergo might well be seen as futile. Yet, dissolution of the boundaries of the self, as bounded by the ego, into greater awareness may be a genuine spiritual path. The Buddha recognized a variety of spiritual paths after death. 'Some people are born on this earth; those who do evil are reborn in hell; the righteous go to heaven; but those who are pure reach Nirvana' (paragraph 126 *Dhammapada*).

The heavenly spirits recognised by Buddhism are Dhammapalas, the spirits of enlightened ones who have delayed final entry to Nirvana awaiting the further salvation of humankind. While a Christian metaphor depicts human souls as fish within the ocean of God's being, the Buddhist sought to become a boundless drop in a boundless ocean and eliminate selfhood entirely, since selfhood was ultimately considered illusory. Buddhism is older than Sankara's Advaita Vedanta philosophy and may have inspired Sankara in his similar concept of illusory selfhood.

Given that a greater universal awareness exists, it may have a nexus in selfhood, as it seems to in individual human awareness. Is awareness possible without self-awareness? I would contend that it is not. Consciousness must entail the ability to self-reflect in conscious beings.

Buddhism poses a challenge in metaphysics. It asks how we can be certain of the existence of the self, an abiding soul, or of greater awareness in a being with selfhood conceived as 'God'.

From India, Buddhism was taken throughout Asia to non-Hindu countries, including China and Japan. A significant development was the Zen Buddhist tradition of China and Japan, which made use of koans with either no logical answer or an illogical one (for example, 'What is the sound of one hand clapping?') to trip the mind into non-conceptual unitary awareness. The form of meditation used was more Taoist than Indian. The promise was of sudden enlightenment rather than gradual progress.

'Sudden enlightenment means satisfying both principle (*li*) and wisdom. The principle of sudden enlightenment means to understand without going through gradual steps, for understanding is natural . . . He who issues from principle approaches the Way rapidly, whereas he who cultivates externality approaches slowly' (Shen-Hui, Sourcebook of Chinese Philosophy).

Both Buddhist and Hindu metaphysics tend to deny empiricism as dwelling in illusion. The Greek metaphysical perspective on forms and ideas in the Logos as ultimately real is oppositional to theirs. They sought to abandon Logos within at a certain stage. The issue of seeking the perfect resolution and balance between the divine selfhood and selflessness would come only through Christ Jesus and awaited his advent.

Chapter 4

THE WAY OF THE MAGI

That Way of which thou hast spoken to me oh Lord,

As the Way of the Good mind, well made by Righteousness itself,

Where the consciences of the saviours go forward,

To the reward destined for the wise, of which thou art the dispenser,
Oh wise One !

—The Hymns of Zarathustra; Yasna 34:13)

THE MAGI ARE the priests and practitioners of the Zoroastrian religion, following the prophet Zoroaster, a very ancient Persian or Indo-Iranian prophet. Zarathustra is the original Persian form of his name. The dates of Zoroaster's life are very uncertain (suggested within the range of 600-6000 BC), as his teachings were originally passed on as unwritten prayer chants. My own opinion is that Zoroaster was an aeon-shaping prophet who had the definitive Divine Word at the end of the Age of Gemini and inception of the Age of Taurus—this is to say approximately 6,000 years ago and 4000 BC. The next aeon-shaping prophet was Abraham, the founder of Judaism in 2000 BC, the inception of the Age (aeon) of Aries. The next was the Lord Jesus himself, at the inception of the Age of Pisces. In fact, knowledge of astrology characterized the Magi. However, this need not be understood as 'astrology' of the popular modern variety. Much of the Magi's accurate knowledge of the heavens, indeed the theory of the ages itself (being periods of roughly 2,000 years with overlap defined by the celestial calendar) has passed on into astronomy as modern science.

Zarathustra saw the world as being shaped by two spiritual beings—Ahura Mazda (later called Ormazda) the good creator of our good earth and the good mind whose intelligence gave all things form and order; and Angra Mainyu (later Ahriman), the spiritual being, who through wrong choice in the beginning, was given over to rage, hatred, and destruction. It is this specifically 'Geminian' character of Zarathustra's thought that makes me certain he belongs as an aeon shaper at the end of the Age of Gemini (the twins); he prayed to be made guardian of the Ox soul (Age of Taurus).

'Now at the beginning the twin spirits have declared their nature, the better and the evil, in thought word and deed. And between the two the wise ones chose well, not so the ignorant (Yasna 30:3).

Zarathustra saw good and evil as independently motivated in the spiritual realm.
'Of these two spirits, the evil one chose to do the worst things; but the most Holy Spirit clothed in the most steadfast heavens, joined himself unto righteousness; And thus did all those who delight to please the Wise Lord by honest deeds' (Yasna 30:5).

Note that, in these last lines, the idea of the righteous conjoined with the Lord God in the heavens is a predecessor of Christian thought and far more like Christianity than Old Testament Judaism.

Some metaphysical ideas—including, the existence of opposing good and evil forces, the good eventually to emerge victorious in an age of purity (*Frashokereti*); the existence of a heavenly afterlife; and the necessity of a test of and transition to spiritual purity through molten metal in the underworld—came from Zoroastrianism.

Zoroaster's prayers and hymns of praise are contained and preserved in the Yasna. Characteristically, Zoroastrians prayed and worshipped in the presence of fire with a fire altar. Fire was seen as a purifying and transformative divine power. *Atar*, the purifying flame of the Lord, relates to the earlier Vedic Agni god of fire in this Indo-Iranian religion, though here seen as an aspect of the Lord's power and divinity, not as a separate divinity.

'Hear, oh Lord, him who watches over Righteousness, An initiate, a healer of existence. Who rules by his tongue at will to speak true words. When by thy glowing fire (Atar) the two parties are about to receive their due' (Yasna 31:19).

It was the duty of Zoroastrians to dwell in the presence of 'the Good mind'—the most holy spirit Ormazda (or Ahura Mazda)—to practice spiritual purity, and to oppose evil fearlessly.

Zoroaster's means of spreading his teachings was to convert a prince, who, when king, would convert a kingdom. Thus, there arose a tradition of Zoroastrian priest-kings and advisors to the courts, the Magi. This tradition possibly led up to Melchizedek, priest-king of Salem (which preceded Jeru-salem), who passed his blessing on to Abraham at the inception of the age of Aries (the ram); Abraham made his covenant sacrifice with a ram. It certainly included the Biblical Magi (from the Vulgate version and original Greek) the wise kings who followed the star to the manger where Jesus was born.

Zarathustra predicted a coming saviour (or saviours), a particular one to be born of a virgin, from his own lineage. I take this to mean a spiritual lineage, though a later tradition attempts to explain this as his own seed having been miraculously preserved in a lake and causing impregnation.

So it seems that the Magi expected a saviour from Zarathustra's own prophecy, at the inception of the Age of Pisces, and this led them to offer gifts at the manger of the infant Lord Jesus.

> When oh wise One, shall the will of the future saviours come forth;
> The dawn of the days when through powerful judgment;
> The world shall uphold Righteousness? (Yasna 46:3; Hymns of Zoroaster)

Another Biblical Zoroastrian was King Cyrus of the Persians, who conquered Babylon and liberated the people of Israel. In Isaiah 45, he is described as the Lord's 'anointed', the Hebrew word being *mashiah* or messiah, saviour.

> Thus saith the LORD to his anointed, to Cyrus, whose right hand
> I have holden, to subdue nations before him; and I will loose the
> loins of kings, to open before him the two leaved gates; and the
> gates shall not be shut; I will go before thee, and make the crooked
> places straight: I will break in pieces the gates of brass, and cut
> in sunder the bars of iron: And I will give thee the treasures of
> darkness, and hidden riches of secret places, that thou mayest
> know that I, the LORD, which call thee by thy name, am the God
> of Israel. (Isaiah 45:1)

Named long before his birth by Isaiah, Cyrus is counselled by God in Isaiah's prophecy that there is only one God, who empowered him and who creates both good and evil. (The Hebrew word *ra* often appears as a watered-down translation, such as *adversity*, but it appears as *evil* in the King James Bible).

Later in the chapter, we read, 'I am the LORD, and there is none else, there is no God beside me: I girded thee, though thou hast not known me: That they may know from the rising of the sun, and from the west, that there is none beside me. I am the LORD, and there is none else. I form the light, and create darkness: I make peace, and create evil: I the LORD do all these things' (Isaiah 45:5-7).

This takes issue with a fundamental tenet of Zoroastrianism—that of twin beings, one good and one evil. God speaks through Isaiah to say all things are in God's hand.

King Cyrus was an enlightened ruler, who defeated the Babylonians, liberated the Jews, and gave orders for the rebuilding of Solomon's temple. Herodotus provides an interesting scriptural tie in confirming that the gates of the city of Babylon were of brass, as foretold in the prophecy concerning King Cyrus's victory over the city, and Herodotus gives an account of how that victory was achieved. Xenophon's account relates that the Magi accompanied Cyrus on his campaigns and that, in conquered Babylon, Cyrus established the 'College of the Magi'.

In conquering Babylon, King Cyrus and the Magi had toppled the regime and religion of Marduk, who had risen at a relatively late stage to become head of the classical pantheon of Babylonian deities. Marduk was a dragon slayer, who became a dragon-man spiritual hybrid. In pre-Cyrus Babylonian mythology, Marduk allegedly created heaven and earth from the body of a dragon. He was the original 'Beast of Babylon'.

According to Herodotus, the iniquitous regime Cyrus conquered, which had enslaved the Jews, also enslaved all women. Women were sold at auction to become wives and forced to sit one day a year in the temple as prostitutes, leaving with any man who gave them a coin.

Cyrus, as we are informed by Xenophon, was fond of the saying that a good king is shepherd to his people. This seeming pre-intimation of Christ can be readily explained by the fact that Cyrus would have been familiar with Isaiah's prophecy, which includes this in Isaiah 42:27, speaking of Cyrus, 'He is my shepherd'. This can be taken as proof of the legitimacy of Isaiah's remarkable prophecy and contradicts the sceptical scholastic tradition that there were two Isaiahs (Proto—Isaiah and Deutero-Isaiah) whose works were lashed together. This nonsensical claim overlooks that, even in early chapters, Isaiah predicts the fall of Babylon (Isaiah 13:9, 14:4, 14:22, and 21:9).

Also in pre-intimation of Christ, by subsuming kingdoms, Cyrus becomes 'King of Kings'. His edict as given in Ezra 1:1 and also 2 Chronicles 36:22 to rebuild the temple of Solomon is also given by Josephus the historian in a rather grander version. 'Thus saith Cyrus the king: Since God Almighty hath appointed me to be King of the habitable earth, I believe that he is that God which the nation of the Israelites worship; for indeed he foretold my name by the prophets, and that I should build him a house at Jerusalem, in the country of Judea' (Josephus, Antiquities Book XI, Chapter 1).

Not surprisingly, since he was named *messiah*, Cyrus had his own wisdom. The historian Herodotus recorded a saying of King Cyrus that may be taken as a prophetic parable concerning Christ Jesus, in the age of Pisces, though historians have given it more mundane interpretation concerning kingdoms Cyrus wished to subsume. The saying is clearly in the form of a parable, which was the teaching method preferred by Christ Jesus. It goes, 'There was a man who piped to fish in the sea, hoping thus to get them to come out; but when this did not work, he took a net and hauled out a great draft of them; and when he saw them flopping about, he said, "You need not dance now, since you would not dance out when I piped to you."' (Cyrus in the History of Herodotus)

Recalling that Jesus told his disciples to be 'fishers of men', we can compare this parable to Matthew 11:16-19, to which I have added a gloss in brackets, which may be closer to its meaning: 'But whereunto shall I liken this generation? It is like unto children sitting in the markets, and calling unto their fellows, And [we] saying, We have piped unto you, and ye have not danced; we have mourned unto you, and ye have not lamented.'

The millennial overtones are clearly brought out in the following passage: 'Again the kingdom of heaven is like a dragnet that was cast into the sea and gathered some of every kind. Which when it was full they drew it into shore, and they sat down and gathered the good into vessels but threw the bad away. So it will be at the end of the Age (Greek—aion). The angels will come forth and separate the wicked from among the just, and cast them into the furnace of fire' (Matthew 13:47-49, NKJ Version).

A later theological variant of Zoroastrianism was Zurvanism, which attempted to overcome the dualism of the earlier tradition. Zurvan is given as the name of the original one God, Father Time, or God in eternity, whose offspring are the twin beings Ormazda and Arihman.

The metaphysical interpretation of this theology, which I offer reservedly, is profound. Ormazda, who was conceived as the good mind, a Logos equivalent, orders and creates all things in the beginning. Arihman may then be relegated to the other end of time, as the destruction and end of things, impending on them always. It is then, in essence, a struggle between Logos and chaos, or order and disorder, which gives metaphysical weight to each side as equal and opposites taking their place within God in eternity. But is chaos an active force or simply an absence of order?

Traditional Zoroastrians steadfastly refused to admit that God the creator was the creator of evil and regarded Zurvanism as heresy. The 'problem of evil'—its origin and cause and how it can be reconciled to an all-powerful God who is wholly good—has been a continuing issue in philosophy and Christian theology. The most common solution is to emphasise that free will and freedom of choice is given to each human being, whereby he or she has the capacity to err and fall into wrongdoing. Zoroastrianism takes this freedom of choice argument one step back, as regarding spiritual beings. Angra Mainyu (the equivalent of Satan) has himself made the wrong choice in pursuing rage, hatred, and destruction. Likewise, those who similarly make the wrong choice go the way of the evil one and abandon the good mind of the creator, which abides in purity in the heavens.

A later day Zoroastrian variant is Manichean dualism from the prophet Mani (250 A.D.), which equates Good with Spirit; and Evil with Matter. Manichean dualism was disputed by St Augustine, who was earlier a Manichean pupil. I must also strongly contest Manichean dualism, as one could as validly see all of nature and the physical bodies of humans as close to perfect but the human social world as corrupted by evil spirits causing crimes and wrongdoing.

We should view Zoroaster's legacy with some reserve, as a revelation relevant to a bygone age. It is not the truth of the Age of Judaism, of the Christian Age, or of the New Age, but may have had more relevance to the spiritual conditions of its own age. It is worth considering its possible influence on the Judeo-Christian tradition and its definite influence of the Greek philosophical tradition from Pythagoras onward in the 'mind of God' or 'Logos' tradition. Zoroastrianism also prompts consideration of whether good and evil are interdependent or independent and in natural opposition.

Chapter 5

THE WAY OF THE PHILOSOPHERS

'TI TO ON?' 'What exists?' 'What is the real nature of things?' This was the question that impelled the Greek philosophers to study logical argument and speculation. The rules of logical thought were becoming known. The very word *logical* derives from the Greek *Logos*,—ordering intelligence. Gradually they were to escape the folk religion of the old Greek gods Zeus, Hera, Apollo, Poseidon, Athena and Hermes toward more philosophical and metaphysical concepts of ultimate reality.

Pythagoras is the earliest notable philosopher. He sought the divine mind or ordering intelligence in eternal numbers that could describe geometry and the intervals of musical notes and harmony, which he saw reflected in heavenly bodies—'the music of the spheres'. Pythagoras may have been the first to conceive of the earth as a sphere. His idea that numbers were eternal and, in mathematical formulas, could express eternal truths has come to fruition in science, though in his time, he was a mystery school teacher, and mathematics, religion, science, and philosophy were not differentiated. It was Pythagoras who first described himself as a philosopher (*philo-sophia*, lover of wisdom).

Pythagoras was studying in Egypt during the Egyptian conquest of Cambyses, the son of Cyrus in 526 BC, according to the biography of Iamblichus. He was taken off to the Persian dynasty, Babylon, not as slave but in some kind of recruitment of the wise, which included the Egyptian priesthood of the school of the Theban mysteries where Pythagoras had been studying. In Babylon, Pythagoras spent twelve years in the college of the Magi, according to Iamblichus, and, 'Here he was overjoyed to be associated with the Magi, who instructed him in their venerable knowledge'(Pythagorean Sourcebook). There is a definite influence of the Zoroastrian concept of God as the 'good mind' in his thinking.

Pythagoras held that the unity of all in the *monad* or One was the basis for subsequent divisions of plurality. The universal *monad*, or God, exhibited an ordering intelligence—Logos (which arose from division into two)—and that a human being was the microcosm of this greater system. The interaction of the limited and the unlimited, or the bounded and the boundless, formed all the phenomena of nature—the limited being the bounds of all things and the unlimited expressed in their myriad diversity.

There is also possible Hindu influence in Pythagoras's thought, as he taught transmigration of the soul though animal incarnations, a form of the reincarnation belief, and practiced vegetarianism. This influence possibly came from Brahmin in the College of the Magi, as India was on the fringes of the Persian Empire.

Pythagoras ran a mystery school, practicing various grades of instruction and initiation. His most enduring and valuable legacy is the 'God as mind' school of thought. He first drew attention to the Logos as the ordering intelligence, both the subject and object of consciousness in the mind and implicit in nature's order.

Pythagoras taught in Greece and Italy around 500 BC. He taught in some secrecy, and only fragments of his original writings survived. We know of him mostly through his successors.

'God is one; and he himself does not as some suppose, exist outside the world, but in it, he being wholly present in the entire circle, and beholding all generations, being the regulating ingredient of the ages, and the administrator of his own powers and works, the first principle of all things, the light of heaven, and father of all, the intelligence and animating soul of the universe, the movement of all orbits.' This statement of Pythagorean belief was given by Justin Martyr, an early father of the Greek Christian church, who held the view that Pythagoras and other philosophers of his line were Christians before Christ. (from Pythagorean Sourcebook)

Pythagoras was, in many respects, a variety of shaman. He taught that the air was full of souls and that souls could travel free of the body. He considered himself a divine being. 'Let reason (Logos), the gift Divine, be thy highest guide; Then should you be separated from the body, and soar in the aether, You will be imperishable, a divinity, a mortal no more' (*The Golden Verses of Pythagoras*, Pythagorean Sourcebook).

Heraclitus, who lived around 500 BC and was probably a student of Pythagoras, wrote also of the Logos and of God (rather than 'the gods') as a unity containing and uniting all opposites. He believed in eternal change, and his philosophy parallels the Taoists of that era. The saying, 'You cannot step in the same river twice,' is attributed to him; he believed all things were in a state of flux.

Heraclitus wrote, 'The way of man has no wisdom, but that of God has.'(History of Western Philosophy)

Parmenides, in opposition, said that whatever is real has duration and whatever is recalled exists, so that there is no change. This may be seen as true from the perspective of an eternal unity. The only true being is 'the One', and opposites are not real; since cold is absence of heat, darkness absence of light, only one quality is real. Parmenides wrote of two ways—'the Way of truth' and the 'the Way of opinion'. He may have been the first to discuss the possibility of an infinite God, which has been common in Christian theology, though it is nowhere to be found in the Bible (in Plato's *Parmenides*).

The Greek word *hodos* for 'Way' appears in the original version of the New Testament, where Christ says, 'I am the Way, the Truth, and the Life: no man cometh unto the Father, but by Me' (John 14:6). Likewise, in John chapter one, the pre-incarnate Christ, one with God from the beginning, is identified as the 'Logos,' inadequately translated as 'Word' in most Bibles and better understood as the divine ordering intelligence, the mind of God.

Restoring the Greek word 'Logos' to the original we read, 'In the beginning was the Logos, and the Logos was with God, and the Logos was God. The same was in the beginning with God. All things were made by him; and without him was not anything made that was made' (John 1:1-3).The passage goes on to speak of the Logos incarnate in Christ Jesus.

Heraclitus had seen opposites as engaged in conflict regulated by divine justice and called this principle 'Strife'. Later, Empedocles (440 BC) wrote of Love and Strife; Love was the unifying principle uniting all things creatively versus Strife, the disorderer. His remarkably clear vision of <u>Love as principle</u> seems to have no earlier precedent, though Aristotle hearkens back to the poet Hesiod for a forerunner in 'The Metaphysics'.

Empedocles also had finalised the elemental view of matter as composed of earth, air, fire, and water, which, in combination within the aether, composed all material things. This provided the basis of alchemical thought for well over a millennia. Empedocles had a reputation as a wonder worker and claimed divinity. He is reputed to have died by flinging himself into a volcano at Mt Etna to prove he was immortal.

Socrates established a tradition of philosophical reasoning through dialectical argument, which he distinguished from rhetoric. He and his followers would question prominent citizens in the market, holding their basic assumptions up to scrutiny (which was not always welcomed). The Socratic method approaches a problem without assumptions, as if in ignorance of common assumptions.

Socrates had a maxim that can be stated, 'No one sins of their own volition.' It had more obvious meaning in Greek, where the word for sin, *hamartano*, means something like, 'to make an error or mistake.' It is the same word as used for 'sin' in the original New Testament. We know of Socrates through the writings of Plato and Aristotle. His death sentence for corruption of youth and impiety may have been partly linked to his talk of God in contravention of the state religion. He also seems to have been a lover of his male pupils. He was allowed to drink hemlock as an optional death.

The sympathy Socrates' death evoked helped Plato to gather funds and establish 'The Academy' for the study of philosophy (from which the word *academic* derives). Philosophy had escaped the marketplace.

Socrates may have instructed Plato in the idea of eternal forms, which he is credited with in the *Parmenides* dialogue (Plato). Parmenides asks if even grass or dirt have eternal forms. Socrates, much his junior, says he does not think so, whereupon Parmenides says that, when Socrates grows older, he may learn to value common things. This is richly funny when we consider that it was said of the very man who, when his student, Xenophon, questioned the Delphic Oracle (an institution for over 500 years in ancient Greece) was told 'No-one is wiser than Socrates'.

In Plato, the 'God as mind' line of thinking developed fully fledged into the world of Ideas or eternal Forms in the mind of God (this is the neo-Platonic Interpretation). In this thinking, physical objects are mere shadows of this divine reality of Forms in the mind of God. The famous cave analogy likens humans to dwellers in a cave seeing only the shadows of reality outside. Its direct predecessor is Pythagoras and his view of the divine and eternal nature of numbers and geometric figures.

To Plato, that which is eternal and true is to be apprehended only by reason, not through the senses. Plato's notion of eternal forms or ideas seems credible when applied to such forms as a sphere, but he later came to focus on idealised geometric forms identified with the four elementals, the platonic solids.

Aristotle, who was Plato's pupil in the academy for twenty years until 348 BC, modified Plato by softening his view. Thus, universals, such as forms or ideas, were only real and having substance in particulars. By universals, Aristotle meant all universal properties, such as roundness, hardness, or smoothness, but considering such properties as 'sphericality' involves forms.

That is, for Plato, the idea or form of a sphere is thought more real than an individual brass sphere (since 'the sphere' is eternal and its many petty examples are transient). But for Aristotle, the idea of a sphere only finds reality in individual spherical forms. God gives all things form and substance, without which they have no being, so that all things find their being in God. The view of substance here is a plastic substrate without form. In the modern atomic view, form is implicit in substance. Yet matter still involves the union of form and substance.

In the *Nicomachean Ethics*, Aristotle set out the case for a balanced good—his 'doctrine of the mean': 'That moral virtue is a mean, then, and in what sense it is so, and that it is a mean between two vices, the one involving excess, the other deficiency, and that it is such because its character is to aim at what is intermediate in passions and in actions, has been sufficiently stated. Hence also it is no easy task to be good. For in everything it is no easy task to find the middle.' (*Nicomachean Ethics*)

He argued that God was the unmoved mover, who was the first cause of motion and who precipitated the transition of all things from potentiality to actuality. Aristotle's metaphysics was to be adopted by Aquinas. The term *metaphysics* (after the Physics, or surpassing the physical) was first applied to a section of Aristotle's works by a cataloguer in the Library of Alexandria.

Aristotle recognised four kinds of cause—first cause, formal cause, efficient cause, and final cause. Consider, for example, the building of a house. Here, the landowner is the first cause, the architect is the formal cause, the builder is the efficient cause, and the completed house is the final cause, which provides the impelling reason for previous events.

Zeno (280 BC) founded the Stoic school of philosophy. Stoics sought to cultivate courage and equanimity in the face of life. Reason was seen as a divine quality implanted in every individual as seed (*logoi spermatikoi*). It was really a Pythagorean development. In the camp opposite the Stoics were the Epicureans, who saw the good as pleasure.

A remarkable wonder worker who lived in the first century BC was the Pythagorean teacher Apollonius of Tyana, who could reputedly raise the dead to life, though there remains little record of his original thought or teachings.

The Apostle Paul addressed the Athenians, saying, 'For in him we live and move and have our being, as also some of your own poets have said, for we are also his offspring' (Acts 17:28). The Athenians were familiar with this idea from the tradition of Greek philosophy, which was often versified.

The Logos concept was further developed by Philo of Alexandria (20 BC-50 AD), a Jewish Hellenistic philosopher who wrote also of the Logos as the wisdom of God. Philo saw the Logos as the source of eternal Forms.

The original New Testament is in Greek, and unless we regard this as an historical accident due to the persecution of the Hebrew Christian community, it would seem that Christ's message fell on the most fertile ground in Greece and in accord with God's will. Particularly, John's gospel is better understood against the backdrop of not only Old Testament Judaism but also ancient Greek philosophy.

In as much as there is a 'God concept of scientists' today, it remains that deist view first arrived at by the Greeks. This view presents a Logos, or divine ordering intelligence, a divine mind revealed in natural law. Logical order must exist implicitly in nature so as to be capable of being logically discovered and described. This points to a divine ordering intelligence.

When Einstein, the discoverer of natural laws in his lifetime, said, 'God does not play dice with the universe,'[1] 'he meant this: The divine mind shaping and ordering the universe has set down discoverable and logical natural laws, which order all things. These laws are so precise they can accurately be expressed in the language of mathematics as formulas.

---

[1]   This may well be a paraphrase, but a fair one, of Einstein's view.

Chapter 6

THE WAY OUT OF EGYPT

I am the Eternal spirit,

I am the Sun that rose from the Primeval waters,

My soul is God, I am the creator of the word,

Evil is my abomination, I see it not.

I am the creator of the order in which I live,

I am the Word Eternal,
which will never be annihilated, in this my name of 'soul'

—Coffin texts, *Book of the Dead*, spell, 307)

THE ABOVE PASSAGE is translated from hieroglyphics from the Egyptian middle kingdom, 1900 BC. Though such translations are more uncertain than most, this passage seems to contain an equivalent to the Logos as God concept of the Persian magi and the Greeks and, finally, the Christians. Like the Hindus, the Egyptians had a polytheist religion. However, the principal gods are seen as deriving from a single source and unity in the One. Even Ra (or Re) the sun god, who was in many kingdoms regarded as the principal god, has his source in the One and in the Word, as did other divine aspects or deities, such as Isis and Osiris; their son, Horus; and his enemy, Seth.

The Word came into being,
all things were mine when I was alone,

I was Re in his first manifestations,
I was the great one who came into being of himself,
who created all his names as the companies of the gods. (Coffin
Texts, spell 335)

It is worth noting that naming and creation are thought to be one and the
same thing in Egyptian theology—creation by fiat or creative proclamation,
a speech act. The concept bears a similarity to the creation events as recorded
in the book of Genesis. 'Then God said, "let there be light" (*fiat lux* in Latin)
and there was light' (Genesis 1:3).

Many Christians who associate Egyptian religion with Old Testament
accounts of the Exodus of the Israelites may shudder at the thought of
similarities. But bear in mind that the Pentateuch (first five books of the
Torah and Old Testament) are written under the direction of Moses, who
from early infancy was brought up in an Egyptian royal family and educated
as an Egyptian. Consider the well-known story of Moses in the bulrushes
and his adoption into the royal family of the Pharaoh. It is, therefore, likely
that Moses grew up under the tutelage of the Egyptian priesthood.

An aspect of the Egyptian concept of the 'Word as primal God' was the
creative proclamation 'Hikê' as this text shows:

All things were mine before you came into being, Oh gods,
You came only afterwards, for I am Hikê.' (Coffin Texts IV, spell
261)

The classical religion of Egypt was more magical than most; the priesthood
were also magicians who would identify with the divine aspects to work
magic. They would attempt to identify with the primal word and command
in order to enable magical effects.

Now I am Command (Hikê), what I said was good,
and what came forth from my mouth was good,
and what I now say, the same shall be performed,
For I am command. (Coffin Texts IV, spell 325)

The ancient Egyptians, and particularly the priesthood, associated directly the ordering and creation of reality with the creative naming of its various aspects. Further evidence of this is supplied by the lament of the priest of Heliopolis in the kingdom of Ramses II, which reads, 'The land is in distress, mourning in every place, towns and districts are in lamentation. All men alike are under wrongs, as for respect, an end is made of it. . . . Would that I had unknown utterances, sayings that are unfamiliar, even new speech that has not occurred before, free of repetitions, not the utterances of what is long past which the ancestors spake' (Priest of Heliopolis).

It is apparent that what the priest desires in new words and utterances is not simply a new way of conceiving of the world or describing it but a way to reshape it and place it in order once again. This is reminiscent of the function of Logos as the ordering mind of God in which the *conceiving* of things and their *realisation* is a creative event placing order and form upon nature. Words considered as reality ordering principles, as manifest in perceived reality.

In Egyptian theology, the god Thoth was both the inventor of words and writing and the patron of magic. In the ancient Memphite theological texts, though, Thoth was seen as merely the tongue of the one God (then called Ptah).

Many stories translated from the hieroglyphs tell of great magic and miracles performed by the Egyptian priests. The feat of Moses in parting the waters had a parallel in the efforts of a priest-magician who parted the waters to retrieve the lost ring of a pharaoh's concubine, who had been rowing a barge, according to ancient texts. In another account, a priest-magician beheaded a bull then healed it back to life. Perhaps the priesthood, though, became too much like magicians. They were not relating to an enduring eternal God but attempting to manipulate the divine will through Thoth and Hikê for their own ends.

Exodus 6 records the showdown of Moses and Aaron with the Egyptian priests and sorcerers, as they demanded the freedom of the Israelite captives. 'So Moses and Aaron went in to Pharaoh and they did just so, just as the Lord had commanded. And Aaron cast down his rod before Pharaoh and before his servants and it became a serpent. But Pharaoh also called in the wise men and the sorcerers, so the magicians of Egypt, they also did in like manner with their enchantments. For every man there threw down his rod, and they became serpents. But Aaron's rod swallowed up their rods' (Exodus 7: 10-12).

Moses was so much a cultured Egyptian that, even after he had married an Israelite herdsman's daughter and had a son, he neglected the covenant duty of circumcision passed down from Abraham. Exodus 4:22-25 records that the Lord spoke to Moses, likening his firstborn son to all the Israelites and threatening to kill him/them if they were not dedicated to his service. Zipporah, Moses' wife, resolves the issue by taking a sharp stone and circumcising their son herself (which would make many a Jewish man blush with embarrassment).

An interesting question in the history of religions asks how much Moses, Aaron, and the other Israelites learned from their Egyptian exile and incorporated in their religion. A more interesting question in divine metaphysics is the validity of the Egyptian theological/magical view on the use of words and concepts to shape and order reality.

Many a magical tradition takes its origins from Egypt. To make a distinction often made in schools of occult science, magic actually affects reality, whereas sorcery (forbidden in the Bible) only affects the appearance of reality. The latter is ultimately a deception of the mind, since sorcery is linked to the power of the deceiver, empowered by evil, and regarded as evil. Divine magic and miracle, in contrast, work with the power of the one true God and are established in the truth of reality.

What then is the difference between magic and miracle, if Egyptian priests, Moses, and Aaron all believed they drew on the power of the one original God? Certainly the distinction, if any, becomes blurred.

The Buddhist perspective on words and concepts of the mind is that they do shape perceived reality, but this perceived reality, shaped by words and concepts, is all illusory—ultimate reality lying beyond them.

A contribution from the discipline of Anthropology to this debate is the Humboldt, Boaz, Sapir, Whorf, Lee hypothesis that "Language first influences cognition; which in turn influences perception."

My view is that, created in the image of the Logos and of God, we have reality ordering powers, which allow us to work divine magic or miracle, but that these are limited by the original and eternal nature of Logos. If we fall outside of the truth of Logos, we risk becoming self-deceived deceivers. The question of what the abiding and eternal truth of Logos can be answered by the study of metaphysics, and my conclusions are to follow.

Certainly we find in Egypt a uniquely magical perspective on the Logos concept. However, the Lord God would abide no other god beside himself and gave preference to the pure monotheist tradition of Israel as the more true, leading his chosen people out of Egypt.

In the Jewish calendar, the Passover acts as a commemoration of the Israelite's exodus out of Egyptian bondage. Jesus Christ also spent some of his early childhood and, perhaps, education in Egypt to flee Herod's persecution.

'And was there until the death of Herod: that it might be fulfilled which was spoken by the Lord of the prophet, saying "Out of Egypt have I called my son"' (Matthew 2:15).

In the time of Christ, Egypt was a Roman-held province. Cleopatra and Mark Anthony, who had resisted the might of Rome, had lost a major sea campaign in the battle of Actium to Octavius in 30 BC, and the great library of Alexandria was destroyed in flames. They had been betrayed by Herod, who had earlier allied with them but shifted his alliance back to Rome.

The significance of Egypt to the history of Metaphysics was noted by Marcellinus—
'If anyone in the earnestness of his intellect wishes to apply himself to the various branches of divine knowledge, or to the examination of metaphysics, he will find that the whole world owes this kind of learning to Egypt' (Ammianus Marcellinus, fourth century AD).

Primarily, the Egypt referred to by Marcellinus was Alexandria, named after its founder, Alexander the Great, a former pupil of Aristotle's, who invaded Egypt in 332 BC. Alexandria was the focus of the Hellenized (Greek) part of Egypt, which was once a world centre of divine metaphysics because, there, Metaphysicians assembled the Greek philosophical tradition with Judaism; Kabbalism; Greek, Indian, Zoroastrian, and Egyptian religion; and, at a certain stage, Christianity. The great library of Alexandria was the world's largest in the Hellenized period and was built up further under Cleopatra, but it was destroyed in subsequent invasions.

Hermeticism and Gnosticism were two schools of syncretic wisdom founded in Alexandria. *Gnosticism* derives from *gnosis* (divine knowledge). Gnostics were believers in direct divine revelation. A body of scriptures—The Nag Hammadi Library—was discovered preserved in a jar in 1945 in Egypt. These include the Gnostic gospels, which tell stories of Christ's life and teachings. The gospel of Thomas is one of these, and it gives a metaphysical dimension to Christ's teachings, where Jesus instructs in a metaphysical and mystical union of opposites.

Jesus looked upon some babies nursing. He said to his disciples,

These nursing babes are like those who enter my Kingdom.

They said to him, 'Then shall we enter the kingdom as babies?'

Jesus said to them, 'When you make the two into one, when you make the innermost as the outermost, and the outermost as the innermost, and the one above as the one below; and when you unite the male and the female as a single one, you will take on new eyes and members of the body and a new image in place of the old. Then you shall enter my Kingdom.'

Jesus said, 'I shall choose you, one from a thousand, and two from ten thousand and you will stand as a single one.' (Gospel of Thomas, versus 22 and 23, agnoi's version)

Compare the following scriptures from the Bible cannon, while noting it is from the Pauline Epistles, thus from Paul, who received his teachings from direct divine inspiration: 'There is neither male nor female for you are all one in Christ Jesus' (Galatians 3:28).Concerning a greater body we read 'So we being many are one body in Christ, and individually members of one another' (Romans 12:5).

The Gospel of Thomas is ascribed to Thomas the apostle. Whether the Gnostic gospels are historical accounts of Jesus Christ's contemporaries or not may be a side issue. Gnostics often point out that Paul never met the living person of Jesus but was converted through a revelation experience on the road to Damascus. He was author of all the Pauline epistles in the New Testament and is counted a founder of Gnosticism. The later Gnostics, however, were a diverse bunch, and the Council of Nicea found many of their writings heretical.

Hermeticism takes its name from Hermes (Greek god of wisdom), and some of its principle texts are ascribed to his inspiration. There is, however, a monotheist belief in one all-embracing God revealed in them. Consider these Hermetic passages:

> All things have been derived from One. (*The Emerald Tablet* of Hermes)

> A God composed of the Unity of all being is described by the following verse.
> He in His unity is all things; so that we must either call all things by His name, or call Him by the names of all things. (*Corpus Hermeticum*)

These teachings are quite consistent with Christianity but describe an all-encompassing and omnipresent God, a metaphysical panentheist view of God:

> There is nothing that stands fast, nothing fixed, nothing free from change, among the things which come into being, neither among those in heaven nor among those on the earth. God alone stands unmoved, and with good reason; for He is self-contained, and self-derived, and wholly self-centred, and in Him is no deficiency or imperfection. He stands fast in virtue of His own immobility, nor

can He be moved by any force impinging on Him from without, seeing that in Him are all things, and that it is He alone that is in all things. (*Corpus Hermeticum*)

The Hermetic doctrines provided a basis for a tradition of Hermetic magic.

If all things are ultimately interconnected and unified, then events in one system influence all events in the larger system, according to the Hermetic axiom, 'As above so below, as below so above.' The mind of the individual is incorporated in the divine mind, so that working with an understanding of natural law, the Hermetic Sages thought that miracles or magic could be accomplished. All things are one, and the one is in all things, knowing this it was believed possible to act as God.

Chapter 7

DRUIDISM:
PREPARING THE WAY

God! Impart thy Strength,

And in that strength, Reason;

And in that Reason, Knowledge;

And in Knowledge, Justice;

And in Justice, the Love of it;

And in Love, the Love of everything;

And in the Love of everything, the love of God.

—"Gorsedd Prayer"-Talhaiarn

THE CELTIC PEOPLES were a civilisation and race that spread throughout Europe. The original inhabitants of Britain, Ireland, Scotland, Wales, and France were Celtic, a people who may have had earlier migrated across Europe.

Our information on early Celtic civilisation is sketchy, deriving largely from archaeological sources, where Romanophile archaeologists contribute their own bizarre imagination to just how allegedly 'barbarous' the Celts may have been. If the Celts were ever barbarous, they were less so than were the Roman invaders, the Saxon invaders, the Viking raiders, or subsequent invaders, who invaded their homelands in successive waves.

Apart from the Ogham runes, the Celts were a preliterate civilisation, so that what is recorded of them starts with Greek and Roman historical references.

The Celts were known to the Greeks from 200 BC, and their lands were subject to Roman conquest and invasion in the first century BC.

It does appear clear that the centre of the religious and ritual life of the Celts was the figure of the Druid, a type of shaman-priest who would also act as a judge in law. They ritually killed those criminals given death sentences, and enemies of their people—and thus came by a reputation for human sacrifice—but could also make peace between armies.

Julius Caesar (100-44 BC) gave an account of his campaigns that spoke of the Druids using Greek letters for ordinary purposes but having an unrecorded secret tradition learnt by rote which they refused to write about.

Many early pagan divinities and cultural heroes were associated with Celtic Druidism. Among the Celtic divinities were Lud, who trapped and bound a dragon in the centre of Britain; Cernunnos, the stag-horned nature divinity; Brighid, goddess of poetry, handcrafts, and learning; and Belenus, the solar god. Taranis (from *taran*, a Celtic word for thunder) was a sky god associated with seasonal change, Esus was the tree feller, and Teutates was a god of battle.

Eventually, the goddess Brighid was to be Christianised as St Brighid, and surmounting the Celtic cross was the wheel sacred to Taranis. This sacred wheel is likely related to the original pattern of the Stonehenge calendar stones, thought to be very ancient Proto-Druidic monuments from 2800 BC.

It seems that, at some stage, due to the influence of Grecian contact in the second century BC, the Druids were becoming increasingly Pythagorean in their metaphysical outlook. Diodorus Sicilus in 21 BC said, 'The Pythagorean doctrine prevails among them' (referring to the Druids of

Gaul). Ammianus of Marseilles described the Druids of Britain as follows: 'The Druids, men of polished parts, as the authority of Pythagoras has decreed formed societies and sodalities and gave themselves wholly to the contemplation of divine and hidden things, despising all worldly enjoyments, and confidently affirmed the souls of men to be immortal.' (Ammianus of Marseilles in Druid Sourcebook)

The Druids increasingly conceived of a single God in all of nature whose reason shaped all of the patterns of nature and taught the metempsychosis variety of reincarnation belief common to Pythagoreans.

A section of the secret teachings transmitted to British Druidic candidates have been preserved from which the following excerpt is taken.

> 'This is the Druidism of the Bards of Britain, as taught in fundamentals
>
> Question: What is God?
> Answer: What cannot be otherwise.
>
> Question: Why cannot it be otherwise?
> Answer: Could it be otherwise, we should have no knowledge of any animation, being, existence, or futurity, in respect of anything, now known to us.' (Druid Source book)

A tradition of Bards, who set magical poetic verses to music may also relate to the musical Pythagorean tradition. In any case, it inspired later efforts in performance-based song, poetry, and literature, leading up to Shakespeare and Blake.

> Hear the voice of the Bard!
> Who present, past and future sees,
> The holy word
> that walked among the ancient trees. (William Blake)

When Celtic Christianity arose, it had a distinctive naturalistic flavour, seeing God in all creatures, and in all nature. Celtic Christians saw God in the eagle, in the grass, in the trees, and in all beings.

*   *   *

I will take leave to give you my interpretation of my ancestral culture, in relating the sacred Celtic Grail myth, which in some sense, concerns the transition from Druidism to Christianity.

The Fferyllt were ancestral beings of British Celtic tradition, beings who maintained the spiritual heat of the land. Their abode was at Dianas Affaron, the fortress of high powers, where they were associated with the governance of dragons. In Dianas Affaron, the dragon spirit powers were contained.

There, Vortigen built his castle, which kept crumbling. Merlin (the arch Druid, Myrridin of Wales) said the castle kept crumbling because two dragon spirits fought there, one allied with the Celts, the other with the Saxons. Later, Merlin himself kept castle there.

The Saxons were from the German province of Saxony. Vortigen first brought them into Britain as mercenaries. The prophecy of Myrridin of Wales—that the land would not know peace while the two dragons, one aligned with the Celts and the other with the Saxons, fought—was true for a whole age and two world wars when seen in its broadest and most profound sense.

St Joseph of Arimathea—whose house the Last Supper was celebrated at (extra scriptural) and in whose tomb the Lord's body was laid (scriptural)—brought the Holy Grail (the cup used to celebrate the last supper) to Britain. By occupation, he was a tin and metals trader in the Roman Empire, then containing Britain. St Joseph and a collection of Christian-Jewish immigrants, perhaps members of the Jerusalem Church fleeing persecution, established the first Christian church at Glastonbury near Stonehenge.

In some accounts, Joseph of Arimathea was Jesus' uncle and brought Jesus to Britain as a youth. This was the inspiration for Blake's 'And did those feet in ancient time,' now known as the hymn 'Jerusalem'. The first verse asks:

And did those feet in ancient time,
Walk upon England's mountains green?
And was the Holy Lamb of God,
On England's pleasant pastures seen?" (William Blake)

Chosen by Merlin's test of the sword in the stone, King Arthur Pendragon, first king of united Britain, sent his knights on a quest for the Grail. Percival 'the Fool' found it but did not retain it.

The German Saxons ended up with 'the spear of destiny', the Roman lance that pierced Christ's side, once on display at the museum of Vienna.

When he was unable to contain the combatant dragons, and in despair of warfare, Merlin took to the woods, riding on a stag and, to all appearances, mad.

Did competing dragon spirits cause civil wars in Britain and then two world wars, the British ally being the purer on account of the Grail purification? It is known that many Nazis became desperately obsessed with Grail lore in the final years of the War.

The Welsh, even today, have a dragon on their crest and flag, as well as an esoteric Druidic tradition of relating to dragons and their spirits. The Grail myth became subject to many Roman distortions, as the Romans attempted to claim all Christendom for themselves.

Certainly Christian religion was taken within the Roman Empire to Britain, where grounds had been well laid for it by Druids influenced by the Greeks. Prior to Christianity, the Druidic priests already knew of the universal one God and, through Logos, the divine order in nature. For their supreme being they used the Celtic word *God* closely related to the Saxon *Gutt.*

Celtic versions of the scriptures include the book of Kells; the book of Durrow; the Lindisfarne gospels; and finally, the King James Bible, undertaken under the first Scottish Celtic king of Britain.

Chapter 8

THE WAY OF THE PROPHETS

Behold, I send an Angel before thee, to keep thee in the Way.
(Exodus 23:20)

THE RELIGION OF Judaism formally begins with Abraham, the first of the great prophets and patriarchs of the people of Israel. We know little of Abraham's life and thought in a very direct way, since the stories concerning him were only transcribed in the Torah during the time of Moses, long after he died.

It seems he lived in Ur of the Chaldeans till he was given a divine command to depart to live among the Canaanite peoples in what is now the region of Israel around 2000 BC. The Lord God promises that, in return, he and his descendants will inherit the land and become a great nation. Like the Canaanites, Abraham used the name *El* for God, some derivations being *El Shaddai* (God most high) and, later, *Elohim* (angelic beings one with the Lord God). These names are found in the Hebrew original of the Torah. Much later, while suffering on the cross, the Lord Jesus would refer to God as *Eloi* (my God) (Mark 15:34). This is one of the only verses that preserves Christ's original language from the same language root 'El'. A section of the Book of Daniel in the Aramaic original uses *Elahh* for God.

Following his victory in battle, Abraham was blessed by Melchizedek, a priest-king of Salem (this being the earlier name of *Jeru-Salem*), whom he tithed as a priest (Genesis 14:18-20). This may represent the transmission of the covenant of the Zoroastrian priest-kings. In anticipation of Christ's covenant (Christ is called a high priest of the order of Melchizedek; Hebrews 5, 6, and 7), bread and wine were ritually shared.

A physical mark of the covenant of Abraham is the circumcision of males. We read in Genesis 17:10, 'This is my covenant which you shall keep, between me and you and your descendants after you. Every male child among you shall be circumcised.'

Abraham knew the Lord God as a being removed from man, a being who spoke to him directly as a special sign of favour. Angels spoke to him and visited him in human form. The Lord instructed Abraham to build an altar at Bethel, though record shows that his grandson, Jacob (Yisrael), named the place. Abraham was prepared to sacrifice his own son to cement the covenant but was offered a ram as substitute.

Ishmael, Abraham's first son through his wife, Sarah's, Egyptian handmaid, Hagar, was in line to inherit the land of Israel (the Islamic Arabs are Ishmael's descendants), along with Isaac's lineage. The covenant was, however, renewed with his son, Isaac, and again with his grandson, Jacob, who wrestled the angel Peniel (face of God) at Bethel and was referred to by him as Yisrael (God prevails), a name later confirmed by the Lord himself. Angel names of the Hebrews characteristically contained 'El' (God) and Jabob may have forged the first Judaic angel covenant which explains certain astonishing references.

'The portion of Jacob is not like them: for he is the former of all things; and Israel is the rod of his inheritance: The LORD of hosts is his name' (Jeremiah 10:16).[2]

Jacob also built an altar at Bethel, a place he named after a dream in which angels ascended and descended upon a ladder there with the Lord above, near the site of his grandfather, Abraham's, altar. We read in Genesis, 'And let us arise, and go up to Bethel; and I will make there an altar unto God, who answered me in the day of my distress, and was with me in the Way which I went' (Genesis 35:3).

Later, Moses inherited the covenant and kept it, reading from the Book of the Covenant and sprinkling blood on the people (Exodus 24:7-8).

---

[2]   Unless otherwise indicated all Bible Quotations are from the King James Version, In other places I have used the New King James Version (NKJV) for the translation of 'aion' as 'Age' rather than 'World'

The Jewish people were, at times, capable of great religious fervour and dedication. In some respect, this is epitomised by the enigmatic figures of the prophets, who often felt called to withdraw from society then re-enter with a divine message or prophecy.

The prophets often spoke directly for God, as if in unity with God, though more traditionally their speaking as God would be interpreted as simply a message they were passing on. Just before his death, Moses delivered his 'Song of Moses' to the congregation. As you read the following words, think of the difference between reading these words as holy writ and the 'word of God' and hearing a living man say them aloud for the first time:

> Now see that I, even I, am He,
> And there is no God (Elohim) beside me;
> I kill and I make alive;
> I wound and I heal;
> Nor is there any that can deliver from My hand.
> (Deuteronomy 32:39, 'Elohim' is the Hebrew Original translated 'God')

Moses was associated with unmistakable miracles. These include the plagues of Egypt; the revenge of the angel of the exodus on the firstborn of Egypt (after Jewish babies had been ordered slain); the parting of the Red Sea; the pillar of cloud by day and fire by night, which guided the Israelites through the Sinai Desert; and other mysterious occurrences.

In the transition from tribal law to a written law code—the Ten Commandments—there was an upheaval. Perhaps wishing to replace the continual practice of live animal sacrifice in the tent of the tabernacle, Aaron, the high priest of YHVH, made a golden calf as a continual votive offering to the Lord. Moses saw that people were giving their attention to idolatry and became the first to break the Ten Commandments by ordering every man to take a sword and slay his neighbour. A slaughter followed, in which the Levite tribe, to which both Moses and Aaron belonged, extracted their share of tribal bloodletting from the other tribes of Israel.

In some respects, the prophets were quite similar to shaman, though with a divine calling to draw people back to God's service and some vision concerning the future. Sometimes they performed miracles.

Elijah performed miracles, which included parting the waters (2 Kings 2:8) and returning a dead boy to life by placing his own body over the body of the boy (1 Kings 17). He could cause fire to rain from heaven on his enemies and did not die but was taken up to heaven in a whirlwind and a chariot of fire. Elisha also had Elijah's command over water; he made a borrowed axe head float in water so it could be reclaimed (2 King 6:6).

Ezekiel (in Babylon) had a strange vision of the throne of heaven landing upon the earth in a glowing whirlwind.[3] The throne was surrounded by four winged living creatures inside a mysterious contraption that resembled a wheel within a wheel. The contraption could fly and travel at the will of the one seated on the throne (Ezekiel 1:13-14). 'As for the likeness of the living creatures, their appearance was like burning coals of fire, and like the appearance of lamps: it went up and down among the living creatures; and the fire was bright, and out of the fire went forth lightning. And the living creatures ran and returned as the appearance of a flash of lightning' (Ezekiel 1:13-14). In Ezekiel 10, Ezekiel seems to identify these same creatures as *cherubim*. However, in Isaiah 6, the only mention of *seraphim*, whose name means 'fiery ones', makes the *seraphim* sound considerably less fiery than Ezekiel's *cherubim*. Simplest they are taken as *Seraphim*. Contemplation of the throne in Ezekiel's vision is the essence of the Merkabah mystical tradition; a lot of angel mythology comes from this tradition.

The Judaic tradition of a single universal God who could never be depicted in images made it an ideal backdrop for developing theology and metaphysics of Unity.

*   *   *

Through the prophets and sages of the Israelites, the Divine Way of God was being outlined in the age following Abraham's covenant with God in 2000 BC.

---

[3]   I have witnessed such a glowing whirlwind in the Western Australian desert.

In the song of David, given by Samuel, David proclaims, 'As for God (El) his Way is perfect; the word of the Lord (YHVH—Yehovah) is tried: he is a shield to all them that trust in him. For who is God, except the Lord? And who is a rock except our God? God is my strength and my power, and he makes my Way perfect' (2 Samuel 22:31-33).

The Hebrew word for 'Way' is *derek*. King David had a particularly close spiritual relationship with the Lord God. His psalms are prophetic, and Christ Jesus referred to them as part of the Torah or Law. The strongest indication of God's omnipresence is given in the psalms.

Psalm 139:7-10 reads, 'Where can I go from Your Spirit (Ruwach)? Or where can I flee from Your presence? If I ascend into heaven, You are there; If I make my bed in hell, behold, You are there. If I take the wings of the morning, and dwell in the uttermost parts of the sea, Even there Your hand shall lead me, And Your right hand shall hold me.'

The Psalms speak manifestly of a divine Way. Psalm 67:1-4 reads, 'To the Chief Musician. On stringed instruments. A Psalm. A Song. / God (Elohim) be merciful to us and bless us, And cause His face to shine upon us. Selah / That Your Way may be known on earth, Your salvation among all nations. Let the peoples praise You, O God; Let all the peoples praise You. Oh, let the nations be glad and sing for joy! For You shall judge the people righteously, And govern the nations on earth. Selah.'

In Psalm 119:1, 'Blessed are the undefiled in the Way who walk in the law of the lord.'

And Psalm 119:30, proclaims, 'I have chosen the Way of truth; Your judgements I have laid before me.'

Isaiah also wrote of a divine Way and made it clear this was no physical path. 'And thine ears shall hear a word behind thee, saying, This is the Way, walk ye in it, when ye turn to the right hand, and when ye turn to the left' (Isaiah 30:21).

He also prophesied a perfect Way to come—one open to the masses, one which even fools could follow without error—in what is, perhaps, a prophecy of Christianity in either the old age or the new. 'And an highway shall be there, and a Way, and it shall be called The Way of holiness; the unclean shall not pass over it; but it shall be for those: the wayfaring men, though fools, shall not err therein' (Isaiah 35:8).

Isaiah indicated that the God of Israel was a universal God, who reaches out to all nations. 'I am sought of them that asked not for me; I am found of them that sought me not: I said, Behold me, behold me, unto a nation that was not called by my name' (Isaiah 65:1).

Malachi too made known the universal nature of God as father-progenitor of all humankind. He wrote, 'Have we not all one father? Hath not one God (El) created us?' (Malachi 2:10).

Zechariah prophesied a time to come when all the earth should recognise one Lord God; this time corresponds to the Lord's millennial rule—the thousand-year day. 'And the LORD (YHVH—Yehovah) shall be King over all the earth: in that day shall there be one LORD, and his name One (Ōechad—Unity).

Many prophecies of the Old Testament prophets may be taken to refer to Christ Jesus. I do not propose to detail these. It is a secondary purpose of the New Testament gospels to point these out. Here is the single most significant one from Isaiah: 'For unto us a child is born, unto us a son is given: and the government shall be upon his shoulder: and his name shall be called Wonderful, Counsellor, The mighty God (El), The Everlasting Father, The Prince of Peace. Of the increase of his government and peace there shall be no end, upon the throne of David, and upon his kingdom, to order it, and to establish it with judgment and with justice from henceforth even forever. The zeal of the LORD (Yehovah) of hosts will perform this' (Isaiah 9:6-7).

Jesus lived against the backdrop of these prophets, and the extent to which the prophets informed him during his life of his purpose is interesting. Like Cyrus, Christ was informed by Isaiah of the role he should play, and he fulfilled prophecy after reading it first. His first sermon was taken from Isaiah, which he announced as fulfilled in his day. In his death agonies, the Lord Jesus quoted (though the author of all does not quote) from Psalm 22:1 in his own Hebrew Aramaic dialect, *'Eloi, Eloi, lama sabachthani?'* 'My God (El), My God, why have You forsaken Me?' (Mark 15:34). This is from the same chapter that prophesied, 'They pierced My hands and My feet; I can count all My bones. They look and stare at Me. They divide My garments among them, And for My clothing they cast lots' (Psalm 22: 16-18). Quoting this line, Christ Jesus fulfilled the prophecy, which, as the Lord, he provided.

Many prophets predicted woes for the Jewish people, and certainly being 'God's chosen people' has not given the Jewish people a great advantage through history. Yet, they were the chosen people unto which Jesus was born.

One prophecy in Zechariah can be taken to refer to the Jews of Jerusalem coming to a realisation of the role of Jesus as Saviour and Messiah. 'And I will pour on the house of David and on the inhabitants of Jerusalem the spirit of grace and supplication; then they will look on me whom they pierced. Yes, they will mourn for him as one mourns for his only son, and grieve for him as one grieves for a firstborn' (Zechariah 12:10).

The Lord's association with the ruling and controlling balance is given in several passages. In Isaiah 40:15, we read 'Behold, the nations are as a drop of a bucket, and are counted as the small dust of the balance.' And Proverbs 11:1 tells us, 'A false balance is abomination to the LORD.'

The Tree of Life diagram of the Jews, though it was copied and circulated at a late stage, probably represented an ancient belief system known even in Christ's time but held secret (lest it be mistaken as a graven image, for one reason). It represented the very being of God and man and contained the idea of a middle pillar balance of the ten *Sephirah*. This was the wisdom tradition known as Kabbalah.

Chapter 9

THE WAY OF THE ESSENES

'As for me, my justification is with God (El). In his hand are the perfection of my Way and the uprightness of my heart. He will wipe out my transgressions through his righteousness.'
(Community Rule 11—Dead Sea Scrolls)

THE ESSENES WERE a sect of Judaism that existed as a reclusive community from around 200 BC to 70 AD. They lived on the shores of the Dead Sea. In the caves of Qumran were found the scriptures they preserved in ceramic jars—the Dead Sea Scrolls, discovered in 1947.

The Dead Sea Scrolls included chapters of the Torah, or Old Testament, which have been used to authenticate existing Old Testament chapters as being in essentially the same form at the time of Christ.

There were also some other writings and scriptures preserved that are not part of the Bible cannon. Some of them were borderline Biblical, like the Book of Enoch, which exists in Ethiopian Bibles and is quoted in the epistle of Jude. Others are their own documents, such as the Community Rule document, which gives us an idea of the character of the Essene sect.

Community Rule 11 gives a significant reference to the Essene Idea of a divine Way-
'As for me, my justification is with God (El). In his hand are the perfection of my Way and the uprightness of my heart. He will wipe out my transgressions through his righteousness.'
(Community Rule 11—Dead Sea Scrolls)

There is some evidence of continuity from the Essenes to Christianity. The Essenes were a purity sect. They practiced water cleansing ceremonies and donned white robes as a symbol of spiritual purity. According to Josephus the historian, they practiced ritual cleansing before the daily meal (or perhaps only before 'the pure meal of the congregation'). It was prescribed that the amount of water used should be enough to cover a man—in other words, total immersion. John the Baptist was very likely a leader of the Essenes (perhaps their 'teacher of righteousness') and decided at some stage to take their ritual water cleansing to the people, which was the origin of Christian baptism.

The Essene Way emphasized spiritual purity; a variety of rules existed to keep members of the community in a state of spiritual purity. According to Josephus, the three main sects of Judaism in Christ's time were the Pharisees (who believed in earthly resurrection), the Sadducees (who believed God gave material advantage to the righteous in life and did not believe in an afterlife), and the Essenes. Both the Pharisees and Sadducees attracted criticism from Jesus, but not the Essenes, to whom only veiled references were made. It is possible, even likely, that given the anti-Roman and anti-Temple orientation of the Essenes, they were a source of support to early Christians, who could not be overexposed for fear of reprisals against their community.

The Essenes anticipated a major upheaval in Jerusalem, in which they would play a key role in some sort of angelic warfare, and their prophecies proved correct. The Essene sect continued until the Essenes saw Herod's temple on the site of Solomon's temple on Temple mount Jerusalem—rebuilt once by Cyrus and again by Herod—destroyed in 70 AD. As Christ had also prophesied, barely one stone remained on another. Only a section of the original foundations survived as the Wailing Wall.

In the New Testament, elusive white-robed figures are mentioned, sometimes as men, sometimes as angels. Compare two accounts of the empty tomb. Mark 16:5, talking of the two Marys going to the Lord's tomb, says, 'And entering the tomb, they saw a young man clothed in a long white robe sitting on the right side.' Matthew 28:3 describes the same figure as follows: 'For an angel of the Lord descended from heaven, and came and rolled back the stone from the door, and sat on it. His countenance was like lightning, and his clothing as white as snow.'

But is there a contradiction? Men or angels—could both be true? Hebrews 13:2 says, 'Do not forget to entertain strangers, for by so doing, some have unwittingly entertained angels.' Angels can appear as human beings but could they be humans of exceptional divinity?

The Damascus document (Statutes, paragraph 15), speaking of the Essene community, states, 'No simpleton, or fool, no blind man, or maimed, or lame, or deaf man, and no minor, none of these shall enter into the community, for the Angels of holiness are [in their midst].'

Belief in angels was important to the Essenes among the three principal Judaic sects of Christ's time.
'But the God of Israel and his angel of truth shall succour all the sons of light,' (1QS 111 Community Rule Dead Sea Scrolls).

Angels may be men and women of exceptional spiritual purity and divine awareness, which enables their spirits to ascend into the heavens so that they have both a physical body and a spiritual body—that is, until their physical bodies die and their angelic forms remain.

This is a beautiful and deep mystery. Of the angels who attended or assisted at Christ's resurrection and his ascension, could some have been Essene 'Angels of holiness'? My answer is yes, for they followed the Way of the Lord before Christ, before John prepared the Way of the Lord for the people, before Jesus Christ opened the heavenly kingdom to his followers.

Consider the first Community Rule:

> For it is through the spirit of true council concerning the ways of man that all his sins shall be expiated, that he shall contemplate the light of Life. He shall be cleansed from his sins by the spirit of Holiness uniting him to his truth, and his iniquity shall be expiated by the spirit of uprightness and humility. And when his flesh is sprinkled with purifying water and sanctified by cleansing water, it shall be made clean by the humble submission of his soul

to the precepts of God. Let him then order his steps perfectly in the Way commanded by God, concerning the times appointed for him, straying neither to the right nor to the left and transgressing in none of his words. (Community rule 1, Dead Sea Scrolls)

These words must be alike to the words used in the baptism of John, even when he baptised Christ. This passage shows both the significance of the Essene water cleansing ceremony, which was a forerunner to Christian baptism, and also the idea of a Way of God that is a balanced path, there being two ways to depart from it, to the left and to the right. These are the two extremities, while the balanced path is in between. In between tolerance and intolerance, in between open-minded gullibility and prejudiced discrimination, there is a balanced Way—the path of discernment and true wisdom.

Chapter 10

THE WAY OF THE LORD

'I am the Way, the Truth, and the Life:
no man cometh unto the Father, but by Me' (John 14:6).

IN THE YEARS leading up to the birth of Christ Jesus, the Essenes practiced a Way of purity through sanctification and water cleansing. John the Baptist, likely one of their leaders, felt called to 'Prepare the Way of the Lord' through general baptism and prophecy.

In Matthew 11:10, as well as Mark 1:2 and Luke 7:27, we find an explicit reference to John the Baptist as an angel, backed away from by the translators, 'For this is he, of whom it is written, Behold, I send my messenger (Greek *angelos*—angel) before thy face, which shall prepare thy Way before Thee.'

This is found also in the original prophecy Christ saw John as fulfilling. Malachi 3:1 reads, 'Behold, I will send my messenger (Hebrew *maloak*—angel), and he shall prepare the Way before me: and the Lord, whom ye seek, shall suddenly come to his temple, even the messenger (maloak-angel) of the covenant, whom ye delight in: behold, he shall come, saith the Lord of hosts.'

The previous passage carries an echo of Exodus 23:20: 'Behold, I send an Angel before thee, to keep thee in the Way.'

It is worth bearing in mind that, up until Christ, there had been no general belief in heavenly afterlife among the Jews. The Old Testament mentioned angels, as God's messengers, sometimes appearing as human strangers.

But the Old Testament provided no explicit promise or orientation that believers could become angels, in life or in the afterlife.

The general belief was that Sheol, the underworld, was the abode of the dead. Some prophets gave indications that there would be a general resurrection on earth, and this was the main form of afterlife belief among the people of Christ's time, including the Pharisees. The Sadducees, on the other hand, did not believe in any spirit, nor did they believe in any afterlife. They believed only that God would bless the righteous in life. Indications of a bodily resurrection are found in the following verses.

Isaiah 26:19 reads, 'Thy dead men shall live, together with my dead body shall they arise. Awake and sing, ye that dwell in dust: for thy dew is as the dew of herbs, and the earth shall cast out the dead.'

Psalm 116:7-9, says, 'Return unto thy rest, O my soul; for the LORD hath dealt bountifully with thee. For thou hast delivered my soul from death, mine eyes from tears, and my feet from falling. I will walk before the LORD in the land of the living.'

Some thought dead bodies would be renewed, but to others, this was a form of belief in reincarnation. The Kabbalists believed human beings would undergo a variety of rebirths (*gulgil*, which means 'turning of the wheel') until the final age (*Olam Ha-Ba*).

Strangely, in Christ's own references to John, we find some biblical evidence that the Lord Jesus himself may have believed in reincarnation, at least in special instances. For example, Malachi had prophesied the return of Elijah[4], and Jesus recognised Elijah whom he calls 'Elias' as John the Baptist.

Malachi 4:5 proclaims, 'Behold, I will send you Elijah the prophet before the coming of the great and dreadful day of the LORD.'

---

[4]   In Hebrew there is no 'J', and the nearest letter is Yod, or 'Y', so that the Roman letter 'J' in English is the traditional transliteration of Yod, though closer to the 'Y' sound in our language. Thus, Elijah is more authentically Eliyah; Jesus more authentically Yesus (or Yeshua); and Jehovah more authentically Yehovah.

In Matthew 11:13-15, we read Christ's words, 'For all the prophets and the law prophesied until John. And if ye will receive it, this is Elias, which was for to come. He that hath ears to hear, let him Hear.'

John, the angel of light, preparing the Way—was he Elias reborn without memory ? Since he himself denies the identification of himself with Elias made by Christ.

John 1:21-23 says, 'And they asked him, What then? Art thou Elias? And he saith, I am not. What sayest thou of thyself? He said, I am the voice of one crying in the wilderness, Make straight the Way of the Lord, as said the prophet Esaias.'

However, the main thrust of Jesus Christ's teaching was the announcement of the Kingdom of Heaven. He promised to his followers a heavenly abode. In my interpretation no form of heavenly eternal life is possible except as angelic beings. Whether he meant all Christian believers or a heavenly elect (the 144,000 of Revelation, 12,000 from each of the twelve tribes of Israel), he most certainly included his apostles, whom he regularly addressed. It is in line with scripture to interpret the Kingdom of Heaven as those living on earth subject to the rule of heaven. 'Thy will be done on earth as it is in Heaven,' Christ taught his disciples to pray.

Jesus was reported to have performed amazing miracles. He brought the dead to life, healed the congenitally disabled, and walked on water. He explained none of his miracles, except in terms of faith in God. What he meant by 'faith' is unclear since he did not speak Greek the language of the original New testament but I would contend he meant something like 'firm will and intent in unity with Elohim'.

In Luke 17:20, we read, 'If ye have faith as a grain of mustard seed, ye shall say unto this mountain, Remove hence to yonder place; and it shall remove; and nothing shall be impossible unto you.'

In other places 'the mustard seed' is itself an analogy for the kingdom of heaven. (See Mathew 14:31, Mark 4:31, and Luke 13:18.)

Jesus makes it clear that you must act in the greater unity of God's being. John 5:30 proclaims, 'I can of Myself do nothing. As I hear, I judge; and My judgment is righteous, because I do not seek My own will but the will of the Father who sent Me.'

Jesus invited men into an immediate relationship with God, analogous to God as father but, at a deeper level, one of unity with God. When first accused of saying he was God, Jesus did not defend himself as having a singular right to do so but instead quoted the psalms.

In John 10:33-34, 'The Jews answered Him, saying, "For a good work we do not stone You, but for blasphemy, and because You, being a Man, make Yourself God." Jesus answered them, "Is it not written in your law, 'I said, You are gods'"?'

Christ cited the following Psalm: 'They know not, neither will they understand; they walk on in darkness: all the foundations of the earth are out of course. I have said, Ye are gods (Hebrew—*Elohim*) and all of you are children of the most High' (Psalm 82:5-6).

The word *Elohim* translated *gods* here can also be translated as *God*, as it is in most passages. For example where, through an angel, God spoke to Moses from the burning bush. In Hebrew, *Elohim* is a singular Lord God, encompassing the plurality of angelic beings. For the truth is, we are only one.

It is logically evident that the exact words of Christ Jesus who read Hebrew Scrolls in Hebrew must have been alike to "Is it not written in your Law,' I said Ye are *Elohim*'" (John 10:34 Restored)

Christ most certainly did not mean judges (the Pharisee interpretation) as he used the verse to defend speaking as one with God. Nor would he approve the inadequate translation 'gods' as if he were encouraging us to be pagan divinities.

* * *

Jesus prayed that all believers might enter into the same relationship of identity with God that he maintained. We read in John, 'I do not pray for these alone, but also for those who will believe in Me through their word; that they all may be one, as You, Father, are in Me, and I in You; that they also may be one in Us, that the world may believe that You sent Me. And the glory which You gave Me I have given them, that they may be one just as We are one' (John 17:20-22).

Since Jesus prayed this prayer, he cannot truly answer it, except as Christ within us. Angelic *Elohim* can answer it. You can answer it.

The rite of the Last Supper unites us with the Lord; by partaking of his body and blood, we are united with him in his covenant-making sacrifice. Through his self-sacrifice, Christ enabled forgiveness of sin as a prerequisite to reconciling the spirits of all beings to being in God with his own blood. There is no way to identify with God but through Christ Jesus (*Yeshua*)—for he enabled the eternal greater unification of God. He exemplified the Logos or mind of God and emphasised the universal law of Love and principle of Love, which unifies in the greater unity of God.

We read in 1 John 4:16, 'And we have known and believed the love that God has for us. God is love, and we who abide in love abide in God, and God in us.'

Identified with the Logos, Jesus is the Logos manifest. Identified with the divine Way, he is the Way

*   *   *

The key scripture I would like this work to point to is the following, from the words of Jesus, the first awakened Elohim : 'Jesus saith unto him, 'I am the Way, the Truth, and the Life: no man cometh unto the Father, but by Me' (John 14:6).

Identifying with God through Christ Jesus means putting on the mind of Christ. This is not self-glorification; on the contrary, it is a form of humility among men, women, and children, who all have the potential of *Elohim*.

After conducting language research, I have amended the following verse, so that it should read better and express clearly the message of 'Christianity', which, in essence, means 'being Christlike': Let this be your mind, which was also the mind of Christ Jesus, who though being as one with God, did not covet to be glorified as God, being content with humble station, a servant among men (Philippians 2: 5-7) (agnoi amended translation).

As first awakened Elohim, it was Christ's mission to reconcile the whole world to being in God. We may see him as a Taoist sage, identified with the eternal and prevailing Way. We may see him as a great Rabbi, a learned Brahmin, a consummate Shaman; as master of all spirits, an enlightened Philosopher and Metaphysician, as a Magi, Priest-King of the Order of Melchizedek. We may see him as the most divine Prophet and fulfilment of all true prophecy, as the pinnacle and pride of all traditions leading up to him, as the master of all traditions. Questions inherent in all religions lead toward their solution in Christ as a pinnacle of divine awareness, and it is this perspective that I have tried to communicate within the preceding chapters.

Let all humanity and all traditions be reconciled in Christ Yeshua-
'Now all things are of God, who has reconciled us to Himself through Jesus Christ, and has given us the ministry of reconciliation, that is, that God was in Christ reconciling the world to Himself, not imputing their trespasses to them, and has committed to us the word of reconciliation' (2 Corinthians 5:18).

The essential message of Christ continues to elude many churches, who hold that only Jesus can possibly be both human and divine. Surely, we must believe that fulfilling Christ's prayer that we all be unified with the Lord God is possible. All are actually or potentially *Elohim* and one with that one, though for many their limited awareness may deny this truth. Perhaps many of us had evil spirits in the Last Age—unreconciled spirits or spirits approaching reconciliation. But in the New Age, we will be reconciled within the one God, wherein we live and move and have our being through Christ the Lord.

The early Christians met in secret to celebrate the Lord's Supper and the agape feast (love feast); they could refer to themselves simply as 'the Way'.

Paul referred to this in his defence before the Jews, in which he attempted to draw the support of the Pharisees, being his former sect: 'But this I confess to you, that according to 'the Way' which they call a sect, so I worship the God of my fathers, believing all things which are written in the Law and in the Prophets. I have hope in God, which they themselves also accept, that there will be a resurrection of the dead, both of the just and the unjust' (Acts 24:14-15).

Chapter 11

THE WAY OF THE APOSTLES

'according to "The Way" which they call a sect.' (Acts 24:14)
(Following Christ early Christians identified as 'The Way')

WITH GENTLE HUMOUR, Christ told his disciples not to fight for his liberty. 'Thinkest thou that I cannot now pray to my Father, and he shall presently give me more than twelve legions of angels? But how then shall the scriptures be fulfilled, that thus it must be?' (Matthew 26:53-54). There was and is no other Way. Christ's own blood was the blood of the covenant, reconciling all beings to being in God. His blood also enabled the angels very being as angels.

On the morning of the third day, though, he arose attended by white-robed angels.

The book of Acts of the Apostles opens with the ascension of Jesus following his Resurrection. He is with his apostles for forty days, 'speaking of the things pertaining to the kingdom of God' (Acts 1:3).

In Acts 1:6-11, we read:

> 'When they therefore were come together, they asked of him, saying, Lord, wilt thou at this time restore again the kingdom to Israel? And he said unto them, It is not for you to know the times or the seasons, which the Father hath put in his own power. But ye shall receive power, after that the Holy Spirit is come upon you: and ye shall be witnesses unto me both in Jerusalem, and in all Judaea, and in Samaria, and unto the uttermost part of the earth. And when

he had spoken these things, while they beheld, he was taken up; and a cloud received him out of their sight. And while they looked steadfastly toward heaven as he went up, behold, two men stood by them in white apparel; Which also said, Ye men of Galilee, why stand ye gazing up into heaven? This same Jesus, which is taken up from you into heaven, shall so come in like manner as ye have seen him go into heaven.'

These men in white were quite certainly angels, though here they were referred to only as men. We know they are angels, for they had a divine certainty about the event that went beyond the knowledge of the apostles, who would in their time also be angels of the elect. They were not known in person to the apostles, so there is a strong possibility that they were, in fact, of the Essenes—sons of light, angels trained by John. Their leader still with them and with the Lord in angelic spiritual form, though he had been put to death by Herod Antipas. They were characteristically robed in white to show the purity they had obtained through the Essene Way, with its spiritual cleansing practices. Jesus acknowledged both John and the efficacy of his baptismal practices with a sideways glance at these angels before ascending. 'For John truly baptized with water, but you shall be baptized with the Holy Spirit not many days from now' (Acts 1:5).

In their physical bodies, the angels in white stood upon the earth, but in their spiritual bodies, they would have been assisting the ascension, along with the Lord's host of angels from all times.

The apostles were human men and full of human error. Saddled with the daunting and seemingly impossible task to reach the whole world with the gospel of the risen Christ, they first gathered to elect a successor to Judas. Peter stated that it was prophesied in the Psalms that another should take his place. This they do by casting lots and elect Mathias, who is subsequently never heard of again.

The Lord himself had other plans and would, in the fulfilment of the prophecy of another Psalm, choose the rabbinical scribe Saul to complete the twelve. 'The Lord (Yehovah) said unto my Lord (adon), sit at my right hand till I make your enemies your footstool' (Psalm 110:1). Christ commented also on that Psalm to identify as adon (Lord) by saying, 'If David calls him Lord, how can he (the messiah) be his son?' (Luke 20:44).

Saul reborn as Paul, would say of himself in Acts 22:3-4: 'I am indeed a Jew, born in Tarsus of Cilicia, but brought up in this city at the feet of Gamaliel, taught according to the strictness of our fathers' law, and was zealous toward God as you all are today. I persecuted this Way to the death, binding and delivering into prisons both men and women.'

As Saul an enemy of the Lord, as the apostle Paul, though, he was of invaluable importance to the Lord and vital in making the Roman Empire itself the footstool of the Lord's enemies.

On the Day of Pentecost, the promised baptism of the Holy Spirit came to the apostles wreathed in seraph fire and causing the apostles to speak in a dozen or so foreign tongues, native to those assembled. Some failed to understand the foreign languages and accused the apostles of being drunk. Peter pointed out that this was not so, as it was only the third hour (and so too early for Peter and the apostles to be drunk). Certainly, though, they were intoxicated with joy and filled with the Lord's Holy Spirit and that of his timeless host of angels. In a paradox enabled by the eternal awareness of angels, the spectators own descendants spoke through the apostles in the native tongues of their parents and forefathers. In our day, with the gift of tongues, people may reach back towards Hebrew and Aramaic to commune with the Lord.

Peter delivered an inspired tirade against a perverse generation. Fearing that they might be held accountable for the death of Christ, who was now made Lord of all and who makes his enemies his footstool, three thousand repented and were baptised. They sold their goods and kept all property in common.

After many miracles of healing, some uncanny deaths of those who cheated the church, and exorcisms in Christ's name, the apostles were arrested. An angel of the Lord freed them from prison, instructing them to preach the words of Jesus in the temple. They did this, to the priesthoods' bafflement, upon the porch of Solomon.

An interesting incident happened in Acts 8. A eunuch who was reading Isaiah in his moving carriage met Phillip, who had been called in spirit to go to the eunuch. After instructing and baptising the man, Phillip was called away again in spirit. Was Phillip really present in body at all or did he just appear in angel or spirit form?

Acts 9:1-5 deals with Paul's conversion. 'Then Saul, still breathing threats and murder against the disciples of the Lord, went to the high priest and asked letters from him to the synagogues of Damascus, so that if he found any who were of the Way, whether men or women, he might bring them bound to Jerusalem. As he journeyed he came near Damascus, and suddenly a light shone around him from heaven. Then he fell to the ground, and heard a voice saying to him, "Saul, Saul, why are you persecuting Me?" And he said, "Who are You, Lord?" Then the Lord said, "I am Jesus, whom you are persecuting."'

The Lord was not present in body, but as Lord of hosts, he came upon Paul with his whole host of radiant angels. The light was so brilliant that Paul was blinded and remained blind until he was healed by a Christian, Ananias in Damascus, led to him by a spirit voice.

In Acts 11:13, a gentile who is to be saved by Peter, was told by an angel who appeared in his house in spirit form, telling him to send for Peter. The disciples were amazed when the Holy Spirit also visited 'as at the beginning' (at Pentecost) and fell upon them all with seraph fringe.' Then I remembered the word of the Lord, how He said, "John indeed baptized with water, but you shall be baptized with the Holy Spirit." If therefore God gave them the same gift as He gave us when we believed on the Lord Jesus Christ, who was I that I could withstand God? When they heard these things they became silent; and they glorified God, saying, "Then God has also granted to the Gentiles repentance to life."' The difference in this convert to the thousands at Pentecost is the Holy spirit with visible fire had rested upon him, chosen by an angel to be an angel with eternal life.

Peter, arrested by Herod, was freed even from chains by an angel of the Lord, and the prison gate opened as if by itself. He thought he was having a vision, until he found himself fully awake outside the prison. In Acts 12:11, we read, 'And when Peter had come to himself, he said, "Now I know for certain that the Lord has sent His angel, and has delivered me from the hand of Herod.'"

Not believing he could be free, his fellow Christians say when he is standing at their gate "It is his angel."
(Acts 12:15)

It is noteworthy that they could believe Peter was an angel in early Christian thinking.

* * *

John had his just revenge on Herod Antipas in Acts 12:20: 'So on a set day, Herod, arrayed in royal apparel, sat on his throne and gave an oration to them. And the people kept shouting, "The voice of a god and not of a man!" Then immediately an angel of the Lord struck him, because he did not give glory to God. And he was eaten by worms and died.'

Paul and Barnabas did great works among the Greeks, preaching and healing. Once after they healed a congenitally lame man, the crowds attempted to hail them as Hermes and Zeus (Acts 14). Unable to restrain the crowds from sacrificing to them, Paul decried belief in the Greek gods as useless, which upset the Greeks. Jews also in attendance seized their chance to stone him, and he was dragged off, believed dead.

The Gifts of the Holy Spirit are best explained by Paul in another passage. Later, he was 'a prisoner of Christ Jesus' (as he says in Philemon 1) among the Romans and produced his best literary efforts in his epistles to the churches he had founded. We read:

> 'Now there are diversities of gifts, but the same Spirit. And there are differences of administrations, but the same Lord. And there are diversities of operations, but it is the same God which worketh all in all. But the manifestation of the Spirit is given to every man to profit withal. For to one is given by the Spirit the word of wisdom; to another the word of knowledge by the same Spirit; To another faith by the same Spirit; to another the gifts of healing by the same Spirit; To another the working of miracles; to another prophecy; to

another discerning of spirits; to another diverse kinds of tongues; to another the interpretation of tongues: But all these worketh that one and the selfsame Spirit, dividing to every man severally as he will. For as the body is one, and hath many members, and all the members of that one body, being many, are one body: so also is Christ. (1 Corinthians 12:4-11)

From time to time, the Greek disciples come across those of the Way who had never heard of Christ Jesus, having only the Essene baptism of John.

'Now a certain Jew named Apollos, born at Alexandria, an eloquent man and mighty in the Scriptures, came to Ephesus. This man had been instructed in the Way of the Lord; and being fervent in spirit, he spoke and taught accurately the things of the Lord, though he knew only the baptism of John. So he began to speak boldly in the synagogue. When Aquila and Priscilla heard him, they took him aside and explained to him the Way of God more accurately' (Acts 18:24).

Paul attempted to teach in the markets at Athens, where philosophers following Socrates some 400 years earlier would hold discourse. In Acts 17;15 & 17,18 we read, 'So those who conducted Paul brought him to Athens ... he reasoned in the synagogue with the Jews and with the Gentile worshipers, and in the marketplace daily with those who happened to be there. Then certain Epicurean and Stoic philosophers encountered him. And some said, "What does this babbler want to say?" Others said, "He seems to be a proclaimer of foreign gods," because he preached to them Jesus and the resurrection.'

Paul made little impression at first, despite having displayed some passing knowledge of Greek philosophy—'For in Him we live and move and have our being, as also some of your own poets have said'(Acts 17:28). But does draw over one, Dionysius the Areopagite, to whom a theological tract would later be ascribed.

A more seasoned Paul later commented, 'For the Jews require a sign, and the Greeks seek after wisdom: But we preach Christ crucified, unto the Jews a stumbling block, and unto the Greeks foolishness'
(1 Corinthians 1:22).

Chapter 12

THE WAY OF THE SUFIS

Then I turned my attention to the Way of the Sufis. I knew that it could not be traversed to the end without both doctrine and practice, and that the gist of the doctrine lies in overcoming the appetites of the flesh and getting rid of its evil dispositions and vile qualities so that the heart may be cleared of all but God.
—Al-Ghazali

THE SUFIS ARE the mystical order of Islam. In a religious environment dominated by Islamic fundamentalism, they yet find a way to be unified in God. Sufis take a broad universalistic outlook at the underlying unity of all religion as relating to the One God.

In the Koran, the Islamic Arabs claim their descent from Ishmael, the first son of Abraham and his Egyptian handmaid, Hagar. Their name for God, Allah, shares a linguistic lineage with *El* and *Elahh*, which was the name of God or 'God most high' to Abraham and his line. It is also related to Elohim (angelic beings one with God) and to *Eloi* (my God), the name by which Christ on the cross called God.

As descendants of Abraham, Islamic Arabs are included in God's covenant to grant the land of Israel to Abraham's descendants. As firstborn and first circumcised under the covenant, Ishmael's lineage rights are inalienable, as are Isaac's. The uncomfortable sharing and competition between the descendants of Ishmael (the Islamic Arabs) and the descendants of Isaac (the Jews) constitutes much of the history of Israel in the last era. God, through an angel, spoke to Hagar in the desert just as she was about to abandon her son and told her to lift him up and from him would arise a great nation (Islam) (Genesis 21:18).

Islam is essentially a religion based on the revelations of God given to Mohammed (570-632 AD). Mohammed was not a philosophical thinker. He received revelations through angels, which were transcribed, it seems, by others. This led to speculation that he himself may have been unfamiliar with the Torah and New Testament except as an oral tradition. Possibly, too, his original revelations were amended by his scribes. The name *Islam* means something like 'submission to God'.

The Koran has little metaphysical content. Unquestioning allegiance to a God conceived as 'other' is its bent. There are few insights as to the nature of God (Allah), who is considered ineffable and unknowable, revealed only by himself or through angels (conceived as another order of being). Islam also recognises *jin*, another order of enduring spirit being.

Mohammed styled himself 'the Slave of Allah'. To the people of Islam he is 'the Prophet' or 'the Seal of the Prophets'.

What exactly he prophesied seems to be limited to the growth of the worldwide Islamic nation under God and to a coming day of judgement. He believed God would advantage the righteous in struggle, and for this reason 'jihad' or 'holy war' is the favoured instrument of Islam and historically responsible for its growth and survival in many battles, where the people of Islam were often outnumbered. The jihad belief is similar to the philosophy of Heraclitus, who held that God's justice governed strife, which was also a belief of the Jews, being the similar to the faith of David and of many Christians.

Certainly if one accepts that God does guide victory in warfare, then the Islamic cause may have had some justice. Saladin had a victory in the crusades in 1187 AD when he retook the Holy Land from the Christian crusaders and established quarters of settlement in Jerusalem for 'the people of the Book', meaning Muslims, Jews, Christians, and Zoroastrians. Perhaps his greater enlightened tolerance gives the justice to his victory

The Crusader state of the Kingdom of Jerusalem (1099-1187), under successive King Baldwins (1-1V), progressively barred both Jews and Arabs from living in the city. The Knights Templar made a fortress in the Dome of the Rock, which they still referred to as the Temple of Solomon, while the Knights Hospitallers protected and sheltered Christian pilgrims.

Even today, the Dome of the Rock (Kubbat as-Sachra) where Mohammed's night flight took him, dating from the earlier Mosque of Oman in seventh-century AD, sits on the site of Solomon's temple, overlooking the Wailing Wall. Muslims believe it was Ishmael, not Isaac, whom God commanded Abraham to sacrifice and that this occurred some 200 meters south of the Dome.

Inside the Dome of the Rock in classical Arabic is inscribed, 'O you People of the Book, overstep not bounds in your religion, and of God speak only the truth. The Messiah, Jesus, son of Mary, is only an apostle of God, and his Word which he conveyed unto Mary, and a Spirit proceeding from him. Believe therefore in God and his apostles, and say not Three. It will be better for you. God is only one God. Far be it from his glory that he should have a son.'

I do not question Mohammed's right to be called a prophet of the one God, for he led the descendants of Ishmael back to the God of Abraham. On the other hand, I must dispute that Jesus Christ was merely a prophet or apostle, as he is taken in Islam, as this overlooks his essential teachings and mission as the first awakened Elohim to open the Way to being in God and, through his covenant-making sacrifice, to reconcile all beings to being in God. As Malachi points out, God is Father—progenitor—of all people, and this is especially true of Jesus, whom the Koran concurs was born of a virgin.

Although details of the angel attending Mary to announce the virgin birth of Jesus are recorded in the Koran, Jesus is represented purely as a prophet, whose followers were Muslim. Mohammed stood up for God's otherness. He argued against the concept that God could have a son and, according to the fundamentalist interpretation, disallowed that humans could be one with God. In one passage, however, the Koran states that God is closer to us than our jugular vein.

A tradition of metaphysics, in which Aristotle is the greatest influence, is associated with Islam. There is also a respectable tradition of metaphysical

Islamic philosophers, beginning with Al-Kindi (840 AD), who argued that no body could be infinite. He said that, if it could, a finite body could be removed from within the infinite body, leaving two infinite bodies remaining. He argued that God was the only eternal being, having no body, and the universe had a beginning and end in time and in space.

Ibn Sina (1000 AD) argued within Aristotelian metaphysics against a material universe composed only of the union of forms and substance. He saw forms as universals without existence in themselves and argued that substance was merely potential. Thus, the quality of existence required a third entity, it was necessary that God exist in all things.

Al-Ghazali (1100 AD) was such an influential philosopher in the Arab world that his attacks on philosophy in the book, *The Incoherence of the Philosophers*, led to the demise of respectable philosophy in the Arab world. Al-Ghazali argued strongly that God's will was not bound by anything and that this contradicts the deist outlook of Plato and Aristotle, who seemed to reduce the will of God to less than that of a human being. He likened certain Sufis to drunken men who would say anything incautious concerning their unity with God and advocated a sober mysticism, though he himself became a Sufi (see quote at chapter beginning).

To the Sufis, Mohammed's night flight from Mecca to Jerusalem and his ascent of the 'ladder of heaven', epitomised the soul's ability to travel freely and unite with the divine being. It is a theme that also has much in common with the spirit travels of shaman or angelic ascension.

Many Sufis have taken a bold stance in proclaiming their unity with God after a mystical or religious experience, only to be persecuted and killed by the dominant Islamic fundamentalists. In this respect, the fundamentalists of Islam resemble the fundamentalist Jews and fundamentalist Christians who would take a dim view of anyone standing up to say, 'I am Elohim, one with God,' whether this realisation (as I contend) is the goal of the Christian life or not. Sufis were often informed also by the Christian Bible, which many had read.

One of the great martyrs of the Sufis is Al-Hallaj, who—owing to his teachings concerning living a life of loving union with God and his bold phrase, '*Ana al-Haqq*' ('I am the truth' or 'I am the real')—was flogged and crucified in 922 AD. 'I am he whom I love, and he whom I love is I,' (Al-Hallaj).

The 13th century poet and Sufi mystic Rumi would later defend Al-Hallaj by saying that the statement '*Ana al-Haqq*' is mistaken for presumption when in fact it is humility to have no being apart from God.

The Sufis were often secretive, sharing their mystical insights of unity in God and religious universalism only in the Sufi brotherhood. Characteristically, they stood a little apart from fundamentalist Islam and took a universalistic outlook. In many countries, they became the missionaries because of their tolerance of other religions, sometimes rising above religious divisions entirely, as this verse from Rumi shows.

> What is to be done O Moslems? For I do not recognise myself
> I am neither Christian nor Jew nor Gabr nor Moslem,
> I am not of the East, nor of the west, nor of the land, nor of the sea.
> (Rumi, 1273 AD)

Rumi also presents an interesting idea of spiritual evolution in the following verse-

> 'I died as a mineral and became a plant,
> I died as plant and rose to animal,
> I died as animal and I was Man.
> Why should I fear? When was I less by dying?
> Yet once more I shall die as Man, to soar
> With angels blest; but even from angelhood
> I must pass on: all except God doth perish'
> (Rumi, The Mystics of Islam)

*   *   *

The Sikh religion of India arose out of the Sufi variety of Islam, combined with the Brahmin tradition, through its first sage, Guru Nanak (fifteenth century AD), who sought a unity of Islam and Hinduism. He said, 'There is but one God. He is all that is.'

The Baha'i faith, which arose in Persia in the nineteenth century, is essentially a proclaimed Sufism that recognises that all religions relate to the one God. This is a saying of the Bahai founder 'He is a true believer in Divine unity who, far from confusing duality with oneness, refuseth to allow any notion of multiplicity to becloud his conception of the singleness of God' (Bahá'u'lláh).

A Sufi tale concerns a Sufi teacher who was contacted by a student of comparative religions. The student wished to question the teacher on interfaith matters. By way of reply, the Sufi sent a lamp and some oil, with the following instructions: If you light the lamp full of oil, the flame burns; if you mix oil and water in the lamp and shake it, it will sputter and go out. There is no need for us to meet, as you may find, by this simple experiment, all you enquire of.

I was puzzled by this story. Then one day, I tried the experiment and found that when oil and water are shaken together they separate, oil on top, and the lamp still burns (as long as the wick is pre-soaked in oil).

It is the hard-line fundamentalists of Islam, prepared to regard practitioners of all other faiths as 'infidels', who contribute most to the conflict and controversy associated with the Islamic religion.

On September 11. 1990, in an address to the U.S.A Congress, George Bush Sr. first outlined a new vision of international politics, in which The U.S role would be that of a 'global policeman'; Bush called this 'the New World Order.' It concerned, primarily, U.S policy toward Iraq's invasion of Kuwait but signalled the beginning of an U.S dominated internationalism.

The phrase set off reactions of horror. Certain sections of the Islamic nation saw the policy as a threat to their holy autonomy under Allah alone. The consequences echo in history as the September 11, 2001, terrorist attack and its aftermath in the 'global war on terror.'

'Oh my God!' (reporter, live at the Twin Towers as the second jet hit).

Chapter 13

THE WAY THROUGH LATER PHILOSOPHY

METAPHYSICS RE-EMERGED IN the Christian era from Christian schooling after 1000 AD and was first harnessed as theology in the service of the Christian church. In the next thousand years, the philosophy of the day adjusted itself to science, before rounding on theology.

St Anselm of Canterbury (1100 AD) is known for his Ontological argument (of the variety that argues that God's existence is logically necessary). In condensed form, it runs as follows: Among beings, there is a lesser and a greater—until we come to that being who is 'greater than which cannot be conceived of'. Now a being that exists in reality is greater than one that exists in the imagination alone. It follows that the being who is 'greater than which cannot be conceived of' must exist in reality, and this is God.

This argument, while it is to be greatly respected, may be flawed, since it does not seem to apply if we replace the word *being* with a particular being, such as a man or a mouse. It may also have led to the embrace of a non-scriptural concept of 'infinite God' (since nothing greater is imaginable) though it may well be that nothing of infinite expanse or measure can be real in a finite universe of limited space or time to exist in.

St Thomas Aquinas (1260 AD) created a unique and highly influential theology through his importation of Aristotle's metaphysics into Christianity. His famous 'Five Ways' are arguments for the existence of God. The first is the argument based around motion or change—nothing is self-moved but moves through another body in motion. This sequence of motives cannot be infinite. So there must exist an unmoved mover, God.

The second is, like the first, a cosmological argument, examining a chain of efficient causes—As nothing has its potentiality actualised but through the action of another and, yet, this sequence cannot be infinite, so there must exist a necessary first cause, God.

The third argument is ontological—since all things come into being then perish, their existence is contingent, but for anything to exist there must be a being with the quality of necessary existence, God.

The fourth is that, in respect of goodness, truth, or any perfection, each exists in forms that are greater and lesser, but there must be a supreme exemplar of perfections, and this is God.

Aquinas' fifth way is a Teleological argument (which concludes an ordering intelligence from natures order)—inorganic matter works toward an end but has no intelligence to be self-directed; there must be a directing intelligence, and this is God.

William of Ockham (1300 AD) was a nominalist who argued against traditional Aristotelian metaphysics and in favour of a free omnipotent God (theism as opposed to deism). He thought that universals existed only in the mind, and one should beware of taking on too many ontological divisions. A Franciscan who wrote a thesis on the possibility that the pope could be a heretic after John XXII contradicted the Franciscan doctrine that true apostles should not own property. His famous premise, Ockham's razor, became a guiding principle in science. The principle states that theoretical entities should not be multiplied without necessity, so that one should prefer the simpler conceptualisation or theory accounting for all known facts. There is something of Lao Tzu in this, as Lao Tzu saw concepts as artificially dividing the unitary truth.

Nicholas of Cusa (1450 AD) had an idea of the nature of God as *coincidenta oppositorum*, the coincidence of opposites; his beliefs were similar to those of Heraclitus. He held that God's omnipresence meant the nature of God was to contain everything, even contradictory opposites. Our knowledge of

God, as it relies on logic, is, therefore, limited, and at best, we can hope for 'learned ignorance'.

René Descartes (1650 prime of life), who was the founder of coordinate geometry, was a scientific rationalist; yet he argued for God's existence. His famous argument, *Je pense donc je suis* (*Cogito ergo sum*, in Latin), or 'I think therefore I am', was an attempt to build philosophical knowledge on a solid rational basis from a sceptical perspective. His enquiry runs as follows: How do I know anything exists at all? Since I think, I must exist to think. Other perceived things seem to exist, but how can I be sure they are not illusory? Here Descartes' hypothesises a deceiving demon who might give rise to illusion. His method is to argue that God must exist, since it is necessary that all perfections have a source. Since God exists, God would not allow us to be deceived. So we can trust in perceptions. Today, this would strike many scientists as an unlikely basis for empiricism, as Descartes intended.

Descartes' contemporary, Baruch de Spinoza, a Dutch Jewish philosopher argued against the separation of mind and body (Cartesian dualism) found in Descartes. Spinoza was dissatisfied with theological accounts of creation, in that it seemed a mere whim that creation occurred at all. A God set apart from man and nature seemed rationally insupportable to him. In a search for a more rational idea of God, he directly equated God with nature or the natural universe, which we can be certain exists—*Deus sive natura*. Spinoza was the most famous presenter of philosophical pantheism, where God and the natural universe are seen as one and the same.

Gottfried Wilhelm Leibniz (1670 prime) was co-discoverer of infinitesimal calculus, along with Newton. Leibniz's metaphysics appears cumbersome, since he rejected the idea that matter could have extension, claiming that it existed only as un-extended *monads* or souls. It is in the Pythagorean tradition of the universal *monad* or God, so that both in the soul of humans and in the smallest microcosmic system of matter, 'the atom' there is an equivalence in analogy. God, a human being, and what would be later known as 'the atom' are all *monads* and alike. Leibniz thought that God gives us 'the best of all possible worlds' but this is a choice among prospects involving '*compossibles*' (things possible at once). The basic constraint for Leibniz is freedom; God, deeming freedom to be the highest good, gives us all freedom to choose. Yet in a world where we all have freedom, it is not *compossible* that there is no wrongdoing.

This is a neat partial solution to the 'problem of evil'; it attempts to reconcile the existence of evil with the existence of an all-powerful being, who is wholly good.

Another of Leibniz's insights held that the actual predictable future was 'a sum over possible histories', that, branching off into the future, there are many possible prospects. He thought the actual predictable future might be the one that resembles the sum of all of these prospects, as if they were averaged out. Steven Hawking thought this a good way to explain quantum behaviour. While we cannot predict which of two slits a photon will pass through, we do know the percentage of photons that will pass through each over time.

Bishop George Berkley (1720 prime) thought that we cannot differentiate between a perceived thing and our perception and awareness of that thing. His philosophy denied that matter existed in its own right, away from perception and awareness. The only reason things continued to exist when no one is around, according to his account, was that they continued to exist in the awareness of God.

Emanuel Swedenborg (1750 prime) was an interesting and diverse writer in metaphysics, spanning both theology and science. His vision of how existence emanates from God differed in that he saw a continual coming into being implied in being itself. All being was continually recreated from within itself. Swedenborg saw the nature of God as a uniting love, present in all creation. He was something of a mystic and had angelic conversations. He wrote about the eternal awareness of angels set outside the ordinary passage of time.

Immanuel Kant (1780 prime) was one of the few contemporary readers of Swedenborg. Partly in reaction, he sought a demystified metaphysics. In *The Critique of Pure Reason*, he presented the theory that our knowledge of the world is not separable from our experience of it. Yet knowledge is in part a priori, foundational, and from the logical mind. Therefore '*phenomena*', or things as they appear, can be held separable from '*noumena*', or things as they are in themselves, though no direct experience of *noumena* was possible.

In another essay, Kant argued that all morality and ethics must have a metaphysical basis in universals and eternal principles or be merely an ingredient of culture. Although he contended with the logic of many traditional arguments for God's existence, for example that existence cannot be a valid predicate in relation to Anselm's argument (previously summarised) Kant thought it necessary to postulate an intelligent and benevolent being in all nature in order to derive moral principles.

Georg Hegel (1820 prime) sought to replace the theological concept of God with an impersonal absolute imbuing beings with '*Giest*', mind or spirit, and becoming conscious of itself through philosophy. His best idea was of a dialectical approach to truth through the reconciliation of opposing views—thesis, antithesis, and synthesis. He had a 'holistic' view, which meant that all statements and premises of an argument must be incompletely predicated, as they need to be supported by a totality of unstated propositions. This meant that all logical argument was flawed and incomplete.

Hegel's contemporary, Arthur Schopenhauer, was much influenced by his study of the Hindu Upanishads. He thought that we perceive the world in terms of representations. He believed in an absolute unity and argued against Kant, saying that we can have direct experience of noumena, but only as an inner experience.

One student of Hegel's was Ludwig Feuerbach (1840 prime). Feuerbach picked up an undeveloped idea of Hegel's—the projection of man's nature onto the divine being. This he developed into a psychologised model of religious thought, projecting the self onto the all in the nature of God. The self then receives this idealised projected nature back through identification. The secret of religions, in Feuerbach's view, was the identity of the subjective and the objective. But though he opposed Christian theology, he could not at the end of the day establish that the process he described as religious *styole* and *diastole* was invalid. As an absolutist, Feuerbach also accepted the ultimate unity of subject and object. He was later to inspire both Freud and

Marx in their views of religion as a superseded form and gave Freud the concept of projection.

John Stewart Mill (1840 prime) argued in defence of empiricism and against scepticism, claiming that we attain certainty in observations through agreement, difference, residues, and concomitant variations.

Frederick Nietzsche (1880 prime) was an aberrant philosopher; in many respects, he was not a philosopher at all, trained in philology and given to aphorisms, rather than reasoned argument. The escape of philosophy from reason had been prepared by Hegel's critique of logic. Nietzsche appealed to egotism and the human spirit in his efforts to replace God with the dominion of a superman tyrant. Nietzsche's abhorrent anti-theology was also anti-reason and anti-metaphysics. His ideas led to the beliefs of later existentialists who saw no necessary meaning or purpose in existence other than what humankind endowed it with, and no doubt inspired the Nazis.

Vladimir Solovyev (1880 prime) had a metaphysical variant of panentheism. There was, in his view, a single ultimate reality—God in total unity, or the first absolute. The second absolute was Logos, and the relation between them was spirit. This corresponded to the Trinity. (In pantheism God is identified with the natural universe as in Spinoza but in Panentheism the entirety of all that exists including spirit is God)

Francis. H Bradley (1900 prime) was a British absolute idealist. For him, an absolute unity was ultimately real and his non-dualist position had a background in Eastern philosophy. Bradley held that we know the world through ideas and the test of their validity was in logical coherence, not correspondence to an 'objective reality.' We may raise this objection: Bradley must, therefore, accept all possible worlds that retain logical coherence (including, say, the 'other worlds' in hard science fiction) as real. Bradley's book, *Appearance and Reality* is a classic of modern metaphysics and begins with a modern definition—that metaphysics is the science of reality, as opposed to appearance.

Ludwig Wittgenstein (1930 prime), a student of the logician Bertrand Russell went through two phases in his thinking. In the first, as a logician, he regarded a proposition as a picture of reality. In the second, he came to regard all philosophy as being merely a linguistic chase concerning formal language rules or 'language games'. He argued that philosophical problems arose from diseases in language. One of my own examples of this contention is as follows: We may speak of a space where 'nothing exists'. Yet how can it exist when it is non-existence? The trick is in the language convention where we treat *nothing* as a noun and the logical problem disappears if we replace it by *'no thing'* exists.

The existentialists gave up not only on God but on metaphysics in general. They saw no universal truths extending beyond man. Often they suffered from existential angst and suicidal depression.

Martin Heidegger (1930 prime) was an existentialist and Nazi supporter who thought philosophy could only be done in the German language (though earlier in Greek). He saw the individual being as bounded by non-existence in time, defining his or her own being, if rightly, then through logical philosophy.

Jean-Paul Sartre (1940 prime), another influential existentialist, saw things as 'being in themselves' and human beings as 'being for themselves', defining their own existence by adopting essentially non—rational roles and opinions.

In the struggle to reconcile Christianity and science, traditional theological concepts of God were increasingly under fire from latter day philosophy.

A problem, which was not fully resolved, had grown out of the underpinnings of empirical science: How could we separate experience from perceived things, the perceiving subject from the perceived object? Or could they, in fact, be separated, in which case there is no 'objective' certainty?

Reasoned philosophy, after aiding theology, and preparing foundations for scientific empiricism, confronted theology, then turned upon itself. Metaphysics which is not only a branch of philosophy but the roots, the trunk, and the fruit, was in decline in the 20th century. The Way was becoming obscured.

Chapter 14

THE WAY
THROUGH SCIENCE

THE 'ACADEMIC' TRADITION of science has its major historical roots and origins in the philosophical school established by Plato in 387 BC, The Academy, where Aristotle was first a pupil then a teacher. Aristotle's work, though it contained his own observations and reasoning, was always academic in the true and modern sense, as he compiled and referenced the works of all previous thinkers known to him. Physics and metaphysics, along with logic, ethics, politics, astronomy, psychology, biology, and other natural sciences, are delineated and laid out in the comprehensive works of Aristotle. Through Aristotle, we know of earlier significant thinkers, such as Democritus (430 BC), who taught that all matter was made from tiny irreducible units called atoms (a view later supported by Epicurus). Eventually, Aristotle would leave the Academy to found his own school, the Lyceum, in 335 BC. There, he and his followers became known as *Peripatetics* (wanderers) because of their practice of walking along paths during meditations and discourses.

Aristotle continued, and included, the important 'God as mind' or Logos tradition of Pythagoras, which we have traced from his time, studying the tradition of the Zoroastrian Magi. This influence from when Pythagoras was in the College of the Magi in Babylon, established under King Cyrus, liberator of the Israelites, and his successor, King Cambyses. In the history of ideas, this is one of the world's most important traditions; it could arguably be the single most important.

An incidental concerning the Babylonian College of the Magi and their influence on mathematics is that, even today, a circle is divided into 360 degrees. This is a legacy of the slightly inaccurate classical calendar and corresponding circular geometry of the Magi, who had a calendar of 360 days to a year. It is now known that the earth takes 365 1/4 days to complete an orbit of the sun. The Magian number system was worked in base numbers of 6 and of 60, which made 6 times 60 (360) an ideal number.

The mathematical tradition of the Egyptian priests of the Theban mystery school was also a significant influence on the thought of Pythagoras and integral and vital in the continuing tradition of science. The priests knew of square and triangular numbers (numbers that could be laid out as a pattern of points in the shape of a square or a triangle). The associated divine geometry describes squared and square root operations vital to applied maths used in science.

*   *   *

A pupil of Aristotle's, Alexander the Great set out to conquer the known world, establishing the capital Alexandria, named after him, in conquered Egypt around 330 BC. The Theban priesthood's mystery tradition was also taken up by Euclid, who taught in the Hellenized Egyptian capital, Alexandria, in 300 BC his thirteen-volume work, *Elements*, which included the chief classical texts of geometry and mathematics in the ancient world, which has had continuing influence throughout the previous aeon.

The term *chemistry* was first used by scholars of Alexandria in the fourth century AD, completing the tableau of the physical sciences. Still struggling to analyse matter in terms of the four elementals—earth, air, fire, and water—accepted by all the ancients, chemistry made slow progress.

Alchemy was not merely a proto-science but a spiritual pursuit aimed at human and nature's perfection through esoteric wisdom. The auric transformation of lead into gold involving the 'Philosophers Stone' (perfected wisdom) and the elixir of immortality were its two most famous quests.

*   *   *

Apart from alchemical treatises, little scientific thought of any merit came out of the first Christian millennia until well after 1000 AD. Jesus of Nazareth, though identified as the Logos, the divine mind of God, had not been a philosopher in the strict sense of relying on reasoned argument and still less a scientist. His analogical parables had seemed to value analogy over and above logic. The conversion of his apostles did rely partly on evidence that, for them, was empirically based observations of his repeated demonstrations of miracles (which may be seen as applied metaphysics). When science did re-emerge, however, it did so largely on the strength of Christian scholasticism, in a tradition of education that rode on the invention of the printing press. Gutenberg's press produced copies of Bibles in the fifteenth century and led to the republication of many ancient texts, such as those of Aristotle and Euclid. Literacy also increased as a result of Christian educational reforms.

Pythagoras may have been the first to conceive of the earth and other heavenly bodies as spheres and longed to describe them in their mathematical precision as a heavenly harmony of the spheres, but in his times, this project was incomplete. It was not until 1543 AD that Nicolai Copernicus described the movement of the planets as solar centric (or heliocentric) and orbiting the sun. Copernicus was a priest educated by the church he published his theory on his deathbed in a book dedicated to the Pope. This theory was eventually to completely supplant earlier flawed attempts to describe the movement of heavenly bodies as relative to the earth as a fixed and stationary point (geocentric) which had been promoted by Aristotle and Ptolemy. One Pythagorean tradition he leant on for support was that the planets orbited an inner fire. The Pythagorean Aristarchus of Samos (300 B.C.) had once canvassed the heliocentric possibility.

Johannes Kepler in 1610, drawing on the astronomical observations and careful records of Tycho Brahe, forwarded a more complete theory of the laws of planetary motion and discovered elliptical orbits.

His contemporary, Galileo Galilei, who had improved the telescope, also published and championed the heliocentric theory in a famous clash with the Catholic Church. In his early work on sunspots, he was criticised for departing from the peripatetic tradition that the sun was in the immutable sphere. Again, when he established that the speed of falling bodies was regular regardless of weight, he opposed an argument of Aristotle's. In promoting the heliocentric theory, he also opposed the Aristotelian geocentric tradition, the Ptolemaic model, and verses in Job and the Psalms that speak of the earth's fixity. Arraigned before a Vatican panel, he was eventually called on to recant his own beliefs with a promise of leniency, which lead to his indefinite, mostly home-based detention. Galileo would have known of the fate of Giordano Bruno who refused to recant his belief in the Copernican system before the inquisition. He also believed in an infinite universe with an infinite multiplicity of inhabited worlds, and was a Hermetic thinker who refuted the Trinity. He was burnt at the stake in 1600.

In retrospect, it seems Galileo was triumphant, since the Vatican could not suppress the truth of his findings. The situation makes a clear case that the overwhelming majority can always be wrong and the truth is determined neither by democracy nor by political power. In his day, Aristotle was so well accepted as to have become dogma, and Galileo was forced to clarify that his on-going debates with the *Peripatetics* did not mean he rejected the tradition of reasoned enquiry coming from Aristotle.

The missing ingredient that leads us to be certain of the heliocentric theory is universal gravitation, which naturally centres orbits on the centre of mass, an understanding of which awaited Newton.

Isaac Newton is best known for his theory of universal gravitation printed 1687 in *Philosophiae Naturalis Principia Mathematica (Mathematical Principles of Natural Philosophy)*. His basic observation was that objects at any height fall to earth and that the same force that drew them to fall acted between the earth and the moon to prevent it being flung out of its orbit and between the sun and planets. He calculated the nature of orbits and the balance of forces required to keep them stable and found that gravity is directly proportional to mass and decreases in inverse square proportion to the distance from its source.

The *Principia* included Newton's three laws of motion, which are cornerstones of physics. The first states, 'Every body perseveres in its state of rest, or of uniform motion in a right line, unless it is compelled to change that state by forces impressed thereon.'

The second states, 'The alteration of motion is ever proportional to the motive force impressed; and is made in the direction of the right line in which that force is impressed.'

The third states, 'To every action there is always opposed an equal reaction; or the mutual actions of two bodies upon each other are always equal, and directed to contrary parts.'

This last provided the theoretical basis of rocket science, as rockets move in space in reaction to expelling exhaust gasses at high velocity. Some thought they would not work in space having nothing to exert force against. It is through the application of Newton's third Law that they do work.

Newton concluded the work, which also treated scientific method with reference to God, as follows: 'This most beautiful system of the sun, planets, and comets could only proceed from the counsel and dominion of an intelligent and powerful Being. And if the fixed stars are the centres of other like systems, these, being formed by the like wise counsel, must be all subject to the dominion of One . . . This Being governs all things, not as the soul of the world, but as Lord over all.' (Newton, Principia)

Newton's other major contribution was in regards to the study of light. He discovered that white light contains all colours of the visible spectrum, which can be dispersed into a spectrum by a prism and recombined to make white light.

He described light as corpuscles. He invented the reflecting telescope, still called the 'Newtonian telescope' after him, and used this to come to the profound conclusion that the stars were distant suns (previous quote). Newton had a Bachelor of Arts degree, in his day there were no science degrees, and his interest was 'natural philosophy' but a review was taking place of all the proto sciences under the Royal academy.

This is the familiar face of Newton, but this studious and serious man had another aspect to his character not known to many modern scientists. For many years, he undertook the serious study of alchemy, conducting experiments, collecting rare esoteric books, and taking copious notes. Newton's other interests were in the area of religion. He undertook an in-depth study of the divine geometry of Solomon's temple and an interpretation of Biblical prophecy that went so far as to make him a prophet in his own right.

Newton identified the Roman Catholic Church as 'the Whore of Babylon' (from Revelations) and saw its influence as weakening in his time. He predicted a 'call to return to Jerusalem' by the Jews in 1899, which corresponds to the beginnings of the Zionist return to Jerusalem movement in Europe. Newton's prophecy timescale had a 'great tribulation of the Jews' ending in 1944; as it transpired, the Jewish Shoah ended in 1945.

Newton was a millennialist believer, and he dated the beginning of the 'cleansing of the sanctuary' and of Christ's millennial rule of world peace in the year 2370 AD. This date is possibly astrologically derived from when the overlap of the Ages of Pisces and Aquarius are to end (the new 'aion').

Newton was deeply religious, though staunchly anti-Trinitarian. He wrote, 'They who search after the philosopher's stone by their own rules are obliged to lead a strict and religious life.' (Newton, private letter, in The Last Sorcerer)

The economist John Maynard Keynes, who came by a trunk of Newton's papers among his estate, wrote:

> 'In the eighteenth century and since, Newton came to be thought of as the first and greatest of the modern age of scientists, a rationalist, one taught to think on the lines of cold reason. I do not see him in this light. I do not think that anyone who has poured over the contents of that box which he packed and finally left in Cambridge in 1696 and which, though partly dispersed have come down to us, can see him like that. Newton was not the first in an age of reason. He was the last of the magicians. The last of the Babylonians and Sumerians, the last great mind who looked out on the visible and intellectual world with the same eyes as those who began to build our intellectual inheritance 10,000 years ago. Isaac Newton, a posthumous child born with no father on Christmas day 1642, was the last wonder child to whom the Magi

could do sincere and appropriate homage.' (From 'In the presence of the Creator')

Although I suspect Keynes may have written to shock, I hope in the context of this work it can be seen as fitting that the Magi should do Newton homage as he revealed the Logos ordering mind of God (The 'good mind' of the Magi) at work in the Universal order, and was the last of the old school of Natural Philosopher Metaphysicians.

Chapter 15

THE WAY THROUGH
LATER SCIENCE

A NUMBER OF scientific thinkers made contributions to our understanding of nature following Newton, and many were secular thinkers. Pierre Simon de Laplace, who did further work on planetary orbits in 1773, was asked by Napoleon why there was no mention of God in his writings. Laplace said, 'I have no need of that hypothesis.'

In 1803, John Dalton reinstituted the idea of Democritus, who worked over 2,000 years prior to him, to propose the atomic theory of matter. Scientists such as Humphrey Davy, working with electrolysis from 1807, were slowly discovering the various chemical elements that now compose our periodic table of the elements. The understanding was dawning that all matter is formed of atoms of chemical elements.

In 1812, a young bookbinder finished his apprenticeship. Though he had never received any formal tertiary education, he had attended public lectures at the Royal Institute of Sciences in Britain, including one by Humphrey Davy. He wrote up his lecture notes then printed and bound them, presenting them to Davy, who offered him work as an assistant. Michael Faraday, a Protestant Sandemanian (a church which shared ministerial duties), first noted how iron filings sprinkled over a paper on a bar magnet collected in a regular array, like the plough markings on a farmer's field; he called the phenomenon this demonstrated a *magnetic field*.

Faraday repeated the mystifying 'Arago experiment' of the French scientist and explorer, François Arago, who noted how a spinning copper disk could deflect a compass needle. From understanding and development of this, Faraday discovered the world's first dynamo to generate measurable electricity from a spinning disk in an axial magnetic array. His discovery of electromagnetic induction led him to the first electromagnets, electric motors, and dynamos. He also had the voltaic pile, a simple battery developed by Alessandro Volta, to utilise and pioneered electrolysis with his protégé Humphrey Davy. The son of a blacksmith, he built all his experimental equipment as he thought necessary. Hands on empiricism had made great advances where scholarly debate could never enter. Science was no longer the province of 'Peripatetics' but of careful experimenters.

Auguste Comte, in 1840, believed that the sciences arose from subsequent stages of theological and metaphysical development in the history of ideas and culminated in experimental and empirical exploration. He first coined the term *positivism* to describe the inherent philosophy of science. The positivist belief is that all phenomena are subject to invariable natural law discovered though reasoned hypothesis tested in experiment to arrive at theory.

Though positivism was essentially a secular belief, it did not contradict the view that these orderly natural laws were preordained by the mind of God or that Logos, as ordering intelligence, is in the mind of the human being and the mind of God. Comte is regarded as a founder of the social sciences, sociology, and anthropology, as he aimed to transfer the methodology of positivist science to the study of human societies.

In the same period, Charles Darwin was off on an expedition on the ship the Beagle to observe nature. In 1857, he published in his famous work, *Origin of the Species*, the theory of evolution. This theory held that species were subject to natural selection through competition and would gradually evolve in adaptation to the environment. His theory was controversial and presented a new challenge to theology based on the literal interpretation of the book of Genesis. With today's knowledge from DNA studies, however, that all modern humans are 99.9 per cent genetically identical (which contradicts certain racist assumptions of the early Darwinists), the theory of monogenesis (that all of humanity descended from common ancestors) is still overwhelmingly favoured. Thus, to a biologist, the question, 'Where was the garden of Eden?' is still sensible, and most lean towards Africa, where the oldest human remains have been found.

Gustav Kirchhoff (worked 1859) with Robert Bunsen (who invented the Bunsen burner) made a key discovery—different elements, when heated in a flame, produced a different colour of light, which could be passed through a prism and analysed. This discovery would lead to mass spectrographs to chemically analyse compounds, and through William Huggins (worked 1890), a pioneer of astrophysics, to the chemical analyses of the sun and stars.

James C. Maxwell's field equations cemented the 'field' terminology in physics in 1864. These equations and accompanying theory offered a new understanding of light as an electromagnetic wave propagating in the aether, a universal medium existing in empty space.

In 1887, Albert Michelson and Edward Morley carried out a famous landmark experiment to test for the existence of an 'aether wind'. This was based on an assumption concerning the aether that it hung stationary in space while the earth moved through it in its orbit. The elaborate experiment was set up with a marble slab floating in a mercury bath on which was mounted a light source, a beam splitter, two mirrors at the angles of a square, and an interferometer at the opposite angle to the light source. The whole marble slab could be turned as a floating platform to see if the interferometer would register any change in the waveform and frequency of the light (which should cause interference patterns) in different positions; it didn't.

The New Zealander, Ernest Rutherford discovered the atomic nucleus (+) and that the atom was mostly empty space with whirling electrons (-) in a spherical cloud by firing alpha particles at gold foil in the early 1900s, giving us the basis of the modern view of the atom.

Through independent studies of the photoelectric effect of electron excitation by light (discovered by Hertz), Albert Einstein hypothesised that light, like electrons, occurred in certain 'quanta'. He arrived at the photon theory of wave packets.

Although today you will frequently read that Michelson and Morley disproved the aether theory, this is not quite true. In fact, they dispensed with one hypothesis concerning the aether—that it hung stationary in space relative to the moving earth. Aether or no aether, Maxwell's equations which assumed an aether still worked.

A composite aether-photon theory might be that the aether is made up of resting massless photons with no inertia, in which case there would be no wind (though photons are presumed not to need a medium). Einstein's photon theory predicted that photons were massless at rest. It is being massless at rest that enables photons to reach the ultimate speed limit of the universe, the speed of light, which is a constant. In Einstein's theory of relativity, it is the only relevant constant and is invariable regardless of the motion of the light source or the observer. Time itself may slow down at speeds approaching light speed, mass increases, and length decreases, but the speed of light remains constant.

From 1905, Einstein made two great contributions to science, which might well have been guided by the metaphysical premise that ultimate reality is the unity of all in eternity. Firstly, he established that time was not ultimately separable from space. With the help of his former maths tutor, Hermann Minkowski, Einstein established the theory that time was the fourth dimension—duration—inseparable from the three dimensions of space (height, width, and breadth in a simplified presentation). To the present time, physicists must speak of 'space-time'. Regarding qualities of reality as separately real serves only to take us further from the truth of ultimate reality as a unified event.

Likewise, Einstein further established that what had previously been regarded as ultimately separable opposites—energy and matter—were united, unified, and inter-convertible. A given mass can liberate energy in proportion to its mass and the product of the square of light speed.

I would like to characterise the thought of Einstein, who (as a Jew) became a refugee from Nazi Germany due to its persecution of Jews, as Metaphysical Judeo-Christian Science. He believed in an ordering mind of God that set out immutable natural laws.

In contrast, a tradition of atheist science from within Germany had set out to overthrow belief in God and gave itself over to a kind of mentalist subjectivist view of reality. To characterise it in extreme terms, the belief of this school of science is that the order to be found in nature is purely a product of the order the subjective human mind places upon it. The result of this is a loss of certainty that the universe has any particular necessary order.

The uncertainty of German physicists reached new heights when Erwin Schrödinger, in 1926, proposed a *gedanken* (thought experiment) subsequently called Schrödinger's cat. In the experiment a cat was in a sealed 'black box' with a source of poison gas triggered by an 'unpredictable' quantum event, such as radioactive decay of radium. The life or death of the cat hinges on an unpredictable quantum event and becomes equally unpredictable so that, until it is actually observed, it can only be described by a probability waveform. Schrödinger developed equations for such probability waveforms.

Werner Heisenberg, who developed the uncertainty principle—that the position and momentum of electrons at any particular time cannot be known in 1927, was head of the Nazi atomic bomb project under Hitler but failed (fortunately) to complete the project.

The Atomic bomb was managed in 1945 by the Los Alamos team only three years after Enrico Fermi (a refugee of fascist Italy with a Jewish wife) first built an atomic pile in an American university squash court. On the occasion of the first nuclear bomb test, J. Robert Oppenheimer, a Los Alamos physicist, publicly quoted (or misquoted) the Bhagavad Gita: 'Yeah I am become death, the destroyer of worlds.' (Its more usual translation is 'I am become time.') The Soviet and Allied Forces overran Berlin before the logical outcome of the nuclear arms race would have seen the atomic bomb dropped there. It was, instead, used to end the war in the Pacific with the Japanese. The 'black box' of Nazi concentration camps was opened, and it was finally known that six million Jews were dead.

Einstein kept up a lively debate with his old friend, Max Born, about the view expounded by Niels Bohr and others that quantum uncertainty places a necessary limitation on our knowledge of events. Einstein was a founder of quantum theory himself but did not approve of the development of quantum mechanics. He wrote to Born, 'Quantum mechanics is certainly imposing, but an inner voice tells me that it is not yet the real thing. The theory says a lot but does not bring us any closer to the secret of the "Old one". I, at any rate, am convinced that He is not playing at dice.'

Einstein, writing on science and religion, supported a deist concept of God as original ordering intelligence but argued against an anthropomorphic God (in the nature of a man) intervening in history. He stated that Judeo-Christianity gave rise to our highest values and ideals. Offered the position of first president of the newly remade Zionist state of Israel, he declined, preferring his equations.

The Big bang theory was developed by George Gamow, Ralph Alpher, and Robert Herman in the 1940s. The observable red-shifting of light from distant stars and galaxies shows they are mostly moving away from us and supports the theory that the universe is in a state of explosion, or rapid expansion and that, at one time, all matter in the universe proceeded from one place and exploded out. It is also inferred from background microwave radiation. Edwin Hubble had first spoken of the 'expanding universe' and determined its rate of expansion. Georges Lemaitre a Catholic priest and physicist had proposed in 1930 a 'primal atom' origin of the universe.

The explosive account is problematic, since what would be present to explode in the absence of matter, in a creation ex nihilo (from nothing) event. My friend 'sea-thru' (angel Rachel) was a Way Divine Metaphysics founder member at 13yrs of age (now defunct Web group). She then saw the beginning as a universe in microcosm in an expanding bubble in a non-explosive account.

"Imagine you are scuba diving at night, what you see above you is like ripples in the timeless quantum vacuum . . . (these are caused by the wave function of the universe). In one of the larger ripples, a bubble 'detaches' itself from the ripple . . . this bubble glows with all the colors of the future galaxies, planets and stars . . . the beginning" (Sea-thru—Telstra Divine Metaphysics Chatroom Quote)

In 1951, Francis Crick and James D. Watson discovered the structure of the complex double helix molecule, which encodes and transmits the genetic blueprint of living things. The spiral ladder shape of DNA made from two strands of RNA, one from each parent, is reminiscent of the Caduceus symbol of two snakes entwined around a pole, an ancient Greek symbol that became the symbol of medicine.

In 1957, Sir Fred Hoyle and William Fowler discovered stellar fusion—the theory that the elements are composed by fusion reactions in the hearts of stars like our sun. Here, hydrogen building blocks are fused into heavier elements.

Such leading physicists as Stephen Hawking now see the task of science as explaining phenomena up to the limits set by quantum uncertainty. The conclusion of *A Brief History of Time* described a completed physics with the words, 'For then we would know the mind of God.' Many feel the task of science is nearing completion. All that remains is coherent unified theory.

It may well be that this is where metaphysics (literally what comes after or goes beyond physics) takes over as specialising in universal and unifying truth.

Chapter 16

THE WAY INTO
THE NEW AGE

The Pattern of Prophecy

The Way, in all its manifestations and understandings, is the individual identified with what is ultimately real—a Way of being involved in the Unity of All in all Eternity, which we can know as God.

In the New Age, it takes a new form, though in continuity with The Way of the Lord. Universalist awareness is a paramount necessity in the New Age to maintain world stability.

The age before us has been a story of the unfolding of the Lord's Way. He identified himself with the prophetic psalm, 'Sit at my right hand and I will make your enemies your footstool' (Psalm 110:1, Matthew 22:44, Mark 12:36, and Luke 20:43). The messianic king, who some anticipated to liberate Israel from the Roman Empire and restore the throne of David, was crucified under the Roman Empire. There seems no way to explain how his dispersed and frightened band of followers should have galvanised themselves to form a religion of fearless and faithful devotees but for his Resurrection.

Josephus the Historian wrote:

> Now there was about this time Jesus, a wise man, if it be lawful to call him a man; for he was a doer of wonderful works, a teacher of such men as receive the truth with pleasure. He drew over to him

both many of the Jews and many of the Gentiles. He was [the] Christ. And when Pilate, at the suggestion of the principal men amongst us, had condemned him to the cross, those that loved him at the first did not forsake him; for he appeared to them alive again the third day; as the divine prophets had foretold these and ten thousand other wonderful things concerning him. And the tribe of Christians, so named from him, are not extinct at this day. (Antiquities of the Jews, Book xviii Chapter 3)

Three hundred years later, the Emperor Constantine declared Christianity the official religion of the Roman Empire; the Holy Roman Empire had begun. The unlikely story of how a crucified man took over the Roman Empire is history. This, however, was only one stage in the plan of the Lord, who in like manner, would rule the world from heaven.

Christ prophesied a world purification to come at the end of the Age in preparation for the realization of his heavenly kingdom.

We read in Matthew:

He who sows the good seed is the Son of Man. The field is the world, the good seeds are the sons of the kingdom, but the tares are the sons of the wicked one. The enemy who sowed them is the devil, the harvest is the end of the Age (Greek—'*Aion*' sometimes mistranslated as *World*), and the reapers are the angels. Therefore, as the tares are gathered and burned in the fire, so it will be at the end of this age. The Son of Man will send out His angels, and they will gather out of His kingdom all things that offend, and those who practice lawlessness, and will cast them into the furnace of fire. (Matthew 13:37-41, NKJV)

Ages turn slowly and overlap; both the twentieth century and the twenty-first century are involved in this transition. Yet we stand at the dawn of a New Age—the next 2,000-year period.

The last recorded prophecy in the bible is the book of Revelation, where a false prophet and a war against the beast, 666, of the apocalypse are prophesied, following from a heavenly upheaval and conflict led by those who desired vengeance.

This was fulfilled in the late nineteenth and early twentieth century when a pseudo Zarathustra, a false prophet, and an intentional antichrist, Nietzsche, (author of *Thus Spake Zarathustra* and *The Antichrist*) arose in Germany. With the blasphemous message, 'God is dead', Nietzsche announced that a superman would arise to rule the earth in a coming age of war. This was the guiding mythology of the Nazis and their Arian superman emphasis; in an empire of *six* years duration, they killed *six* million of Abraham's covenant people—the Jews, represented by the *six*-pointed Star of David.

The Nazis contracted a concordat with Cardinal Pacelli to enable their rise to power by withdrawing the Catholic centralist party. In article 14, this document gave them rights to approve candidates to the office of German archbishop subject to political considerations, and in article 16, it imposed an obligation for German bishops to swear an oath of allegiance to the Nazi Reich. Cardinal Pacelli, earlier a canon lawyer in part responsible for translating the doctrine of papal infallibility into canon law, was to become Pope Pious XII and condone, by this complicity and further silence, the Holocaust of the Jews.

The Vatican I had become the whore of Babylon, promised to Christ but given over to a bloodthirsty atheistic regime. The Nazis were the unholy end of the Holy Roman Empire, mimicking the 'Hail Caesar' of the Romans and the promised millennial rule of Christ in their promised 'thousand-year Reich'.

Yet the Roman Catholic Church contained many faithful Christians and was revived in Vatican II under John XXIII. In the transition of the millennia this Second Vatican Council has had its first non-Roman pope, John Paul II, who made an apology to the Jews for the Catholic involvement in the Holocaust and did much for interfaith unity.

The millennia would begin when the dragon was cast down and bound (to which I am spiritual witness and angelic participant), enabling the rule of Christ and the angel hosts over earth for a thousand years of relative peace and enlightenment. After this thousand years, the deceiver would be loosed to lead those not of the Way into the final conflict, Armageddon. The war between two forces, both imbalanced, Gog and Magog (neither representing good) would lay waste much of the earth, while the New Jerusalem would survive. And the earth would later be restored and renewed.

I do not wish to be a prophet of doom, even in interpreting prophecy concerning the events of a thousand years' time. The Lord does not agree to be bound by prophecy. For example, no one, not even his angels, can predict when he will walk the earth again. It may be that the mountain of Armageddon (Mt Harmagidio, no longer prominent in Israel) has been lifted and cast into the sea. So much depends on the free will of the Lord and angelic Elohim and that of all human beings.

We are entering a new age of the millennial rule of Christ's kingdom of heaven over earth. The Day of Judgement.

'But, beloved, be not ignorant of this one thing, that one day is with the Lord as a thousand years, and a thousand years as one day' (2 Peter 3:8).
On the third day, Christ rose. On the third day, the temple will be rebuilt. The youngest Jewish child on the Passover asked, 'Why is this day different from any other day?' We should each ask and answer this question. It is the morning of the third day.

While the last age was one of separation of good and evil powers, pending their conflict in heaven and on earth, a kingdom of spiritual purity has been established in the heavens, and in universal awareness by the Lord; this kingdom will rule over an earth approaching unity.

Consider this passage: 'But even if our gospel is veiled, it is veiled to those who are perishing, whose minds the god of this {previous} age has blinded, who do not believe, lest the light of the gospel of the glory of Christ, who is the image of God, should shine on them' (2 Corinthians 4:3-4; NKJV).
I have inserted the word 'previous' in this text to indicate that since it was written in the last Age it now refers to the previous age when the truth of being in God as *Elohim* in Unity with Christ was hidden by the deceiver. In the New Age we can know the truth.

Unity in God is the defining characteristic of the New Age ahead. Spirits will be reconciled to being in God or purified in the fire below by angels (the earths molten core burns at over 5000 C). The influence of the deceiver, who led people into the egotistic delusion of being apart from God, is at an end. All that science has discovered of truth is the truth of the working of the Logos, the mind of God in all.

The true mission of Christ was not only to forgive sins, but this only as a first step to reconciling all beings to being in God through his Covenant, as indicated in the verse-'Now all things are of God, who has reconciled us to Himself through Jesus Christ' (2 Corinthians 5:18).

All truth is the truth of God, though we have all made errors and fallen short of the truth of God. The gospel's Greek word for sin *hamartano* can mean simply 'error' or 'mistake'.

The 'Ever becoming One' (a translation of the Mosaic Hebrew Name of God, Yehovah) evolves in and through the world and all beings, toward the realisation of Christ's prayer for us, 'that they may be One just as We are One' (John 17:22).

There is no more logical or practical basis for theology than the belief that God is the unity of all, a theological doctrine that has become known as panentheism. Understanding love as the unifying principle and unity in totality in eternity as ultimately real leads us to metaphysical panentheism.

The following is my own variety of the Ontological argument:

> I define God as follows: God is the All in One, and One in All.

> If anything exists, then the sum of all existing things must exist, the All in One.

> I exist because for me to say, 'I do not exist', is self-contradictory; I must exist to say this.

> Because anything exists, then the sum of all existing things must exist, the All in One.

The One being all is in all, and all depend for existence on the One.

Therefore my God exists, and all that exists, exists within God.

Before the fall, in the sacred myth of Genesis, humanity lived in unity with God and nature; the false knowledge—that good and evil are opposites—given by the serpent, alienated humanity from God. *Good* is in the natural balance of extremes; the balance is enabled by all-embracing love and the unity of God, whose character cannot be represented partially and who is good. Because freedom is the greater good, and implicit in Logos as the first principle, the beings within God have the capacity to err.

Love unites the opposites, conjoining the implied two within the all in one and one in all. Only love can unite the contraries and reconcile the irreconcilables. God is love. Love unites all as One. There is no greater principle or power.

The truth of union is greater than the two, since it recreates the original unity, the truth of all, the truth of God. God's love is implicit in the Logos principle, eternally creating in the Universe through separation and through union.

We are all part of the body and consciousness of the one God eternal and omnipresent in whom we live and move and have our being and in the image of Gods totality.

Yet we must not fall into the egotistic error of saying, 'I am God.' No human can know all things, yet God contains all awareness. As our consciousness expands in God, we may know many things, and we may even approach the awareness of the Godhead. But could one person ever know all lives, all facts, or even how many have died in the world today?

Angels, prophets, and Christ the Lord all spoke for God yet prayed and worshiped.

I have no being but in God, but I am not God in God's totality. I am created in the image of God, but I am not God in God's totality. My consciousness expresses the Logos, the Divine ordering intelligence in all the universe, but I am not God in God's totality. I am included in the all-inclusive, the divine unity of God, the ultimate reality. Yet am I God? I am Elohim, one of a multiplicity in unity with God.

Through Christ, we become members of a greater body, the Body of the Lord. Considering this analogy, could your big toe, if it could speak, say, 'I am you'? Or could it truthfully say, 'I am not you'?

Only through Christ and as one with him can we identify as one with God, transcending the individual ego; this is the Way of the Lord. The Way of the Lord is unity in God.
Christ said—'And you shall know the truth, and the truth shall make you free' (John 8:32).

The following verse points out that as *Elohim* and Metaphysicians we should not focus on the transient but the eternal. 'While we do not look at the things which are seen, but at the things which are not seen. For the things which are seen are temporary, but the things which are not seen are eternal' (2 Corinthians 4:18).

These passages lead on to Divine Metaphysics—the study of ultimate reality and the eternal truth of God, which is the ultimate discipline of truth and enlightenment. Spiritual meat for those weaned from the spiritual milk of faith. Though we all have needed this milk to grow.

Follow the Way in purity and in peace, with balance. The only necessary unity is in God.

Chapter 17

THE WAY IN DIVINE METAPHYSICS

WE AWAKE TO the New Age with a hangover from the old—a legacy of spiritual and ideological disunity. Science has advanced and proven its merit in technological achievement. We confirm and verify the truth of science every day with technology. To be dismissive of empirical reality, otherworldly, or absolutist is no longer sufficient. The stock of the most certain of scientific evidence can and should be integrated with the eternal truth of God, as it reveals the Logos designing mind of God in the Universal Order.

Metaphysics is an integral keynote of the age ahead. The best of religion, philosophy, and science is metaphysics, which expands human awareness towards universal truth. As Aristotle once noted in his *Metaphysics*, every human knows the immediate objects of sense perception but wisdom lies in approaching the universal truth behind them. Any claim to truth is, or implies, a metaphysical claim, and it is within the ambit of metaphysics to test and reconcile the truths of existence into a coherent and universal whole.

Sometimes called 'the Queen of the Sciences', metaphysics takes its name from the writings of Aristotle, who spoke of a penultimate divine science in the following words: 'For the science which it would be most meet for God to have is a divine science, and so is any science that deals with divine objects; and this science alone has both these qualities; for (1) God is thought to be among the causes of all things and to be a first principle, and (2) such a science either God alone can have, or God above all others. All the sciences, indeed, are more necessary than this, but none is better.(Aristotle—The Metaphysics)

While Aristotle's view is well regarded, I expect that metaphysics may become, in this age, the most necessary of sciences, as necessary to the necessary being of God.

In the previous age, there was an apparent retreat of the Christian religion into super-naturalist transcendentalism; 'God' was conceived as 'other', in some separate transcendent supernatural domain. This made theology seem illogical and incoherent. Language and its concepts are derived from experience of the natural world; how could they apply at all to a separate domain? Nevertheless, it was, perhaps, the spiritual conditions of the age with the heavenly spiritual realm withdrawn during conflict that caused this distancing of humanity from God. An age of separation, not of union, precedes us. Perhaps at some stage, only analogy, favoured by Jesus, could bridge this gap.

But analogy may extend into metaphysics, which has the character of analogy, proceeding into universal equivalences, though incorporating logic.

There is still possible logical sense in the transcendent, though it does not rest in otherness but in unity, in eternity, thus transcending the things of the present though inclusive of them. There is also a legitimate understanding of the supernatural (the Latin *superus* means 'passing beyond') including the present natural world though going beyond it.

The logical absurdity of an 'infinite God' still not vast enough to include and involve humankind and nature seems to be overlooked by those under the thrall of old-age theology. Nowhere in the Hebrew and Greek testaments does it say that God is infinite. Yet this concept, an import from geometry and first applied to God by Parmenides, is used as yet another reason to differentiate the human 'finite being' from God the 'infinite being'. In a universe that, at any moment, is measurable in metres (though expanding) and all eternity in minutes, why include the nothingness outside this in God? Can anything exist without dimension or duration to exist in? A better conception is the Pythagorean interaction and unity of the bounded and the boundless, which recognises infinitude even in microcosm and enables us, as the poet Blake, says:-

> To see a world in a grain of sand, and heaven in a wildflower,
> Hold infinity in the palm of your hand, and eternity in an hour.
> (William Blake, 'Auguries of Innocence')

Christ came to create a Way to being in God, a bridge in awareness, not a barrier. Yet some have regarded his Way as impassable. No true divine metaphysics or theology should ultimately divide humanity from God.

There is a case to be made for the logic of 'spirit', which proceeds from the ultimate reality of unity in eternity—God, including all beings equally in all space-time. This will justify the beliefs of the vast majority of people in all times and cultures of the past and assist in reconciling Christianity to science.

Spirit is an intermediate reality between the ultimate reality of unity in eternity, inclusive of all time and space, and the temporal reality of the present. Spirit transcends time and space. We can understand in our minds that the unity of all in eternity includes us and all beings, or actually perceive the merging and interaction of beings over all time and space as spirit.

Principle and eternal law, including scientific law, are also eternal, universal, and of the mind of God. Logical order must exist implicitly in nature so as to be capable of being logically discovered and described. The Logos is the logic of the Way of nature, and through science, Logos understands Logos.

Love as principle unites opposites creatively, and Logic relates opposites, its most basic form being binary.

The Way is nature's order, the origin of all. The Logos is nature's order, the origin of all. The Way is not simply revealed by ideas; as Logos, it is the origin of true ideas—the ideas or forms, principle patterns in the mind of God, which shape the real.

Figure 17 The Key Diagram—Love, Logos, Equipoise, The Way

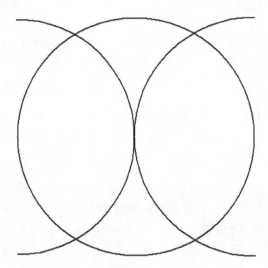

LOVE is first the Love Divine, drawing opposites into creative unity—love as principle—and, following from this, the love of humankind.

LOGOS is first the Mind Divine, organising nature and natural law and, following from this, the logical mind of human beings.

LAW is first the Law Eternal—metaphysical law established by God and, afterwards, the law of humankind. Equipoise is the Law of Necessary balance and equivalence, entailing necessary counterbalance.

THE WAY is first the Divine Way, which all nature follows—the principle with which all true principles are consistent—and, from understanding of this, the ideal Way for Humanity. It is a Way to identify with the ultimately real, of being in God, and maintaining true values derived from this.

These eternal principles all proceed from one—the one principle with which all true principles are consistent. To give it a name we can call it the Way, Logos, or Love; but to give it a symbolic representation, I use the symbol of two semicircles meeting centrally within a circle.

There are many developments and discoveries that await us in divine metaphysics, though the truth always has a familiar feel to it and has been glimpsed before. It has been discovered, not simply invented. There is nothing else to notice other than what is always and everywhere real and true.

The truth is like a lost continent awaiting discovery; yet if we find it already inhabited by those who have dwelt there, shall we then plant a flag and claim the truth as our own ? And is the truth a democracy?

'Democratic but Despotic the Truth feels simple never strange. Together we have dined a spiritual feast where souls roam free' (angel gameloi—Nessa (at 17 years); Way Divine Metaphysics founding member-Telstra Divine Metaphysics Chatroom Quote).

'God alone knows all things, there is no need for us to know any more than we know' (Lady-angel-Jen, esoi (at 14 years) Telstra Divine Metaphysics Chatroom Quote).

In the next chapter, I present my theory of Equipoise, the next development in Divine Metaphysics.

Chapter 18

THE WAY IN EQUIPOISE

THE ALL IN ONE AND ONE IN ALL

When I define God as the all in one and one in all, I am not merely making a repetition. What I mean by 'the all in one' is apparent enough; all things are considered as one—the universal set of all that exists over all time in unity, this unity being the ultimate reality.

The second part of the phrase—'the one in all'—is more mysterious in its meaning. The one that is all expresses itself implicitly through each individual thing, and particularly in natural systems. How this is achieved is through Equipoise, the maintenance of natural overall balance, which implicitly informs balance in each individual system at every level, down to atomic balance. This is a principle of metaphysical equilibrium. The balance of each individual system is not obtained solely within that system but within the ultimate reality of the unity of all. The Way in which opposites attract and creatively unite is according to the principle I call simply 'Love', the Way in which, through contradistinction and interrelation intelligence, is expressed in this operation I call 'Logos,' ordering intelligence

Figure 18 Equipoise—a pattern of implicit order.

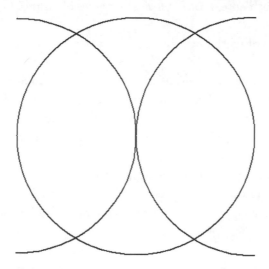

The Two and the One

The primary reality is the all in one—God, single, unitary, and entire in eternal omnipresence. Yet within the one, there are apparent opposites occurring naturally. As we begin to conceptualise experience, we are able to form contradistinguishing categories or dichotomies to analyse experience and to reason from.

In nature, there are evidently male and female beings (which traditionally in human thought represent or lean toward qualities found combined in both); there is an evident difference in perceptions of dark and light, cold and hot, below and above, inner and outer, past and future (though their differences may not be absolute). A whole range of apparent natural opposites are perceived and conceptualised, including energy and matter. Through their interaction, and unity, our reality is established.

Many flirt with the truth, but few penetrate. Perhaps only the most ardent lovers of the truth penetrate the truth, while to most, the truth appears impenetrable.

Sometimes the truth comes to you like a lover; then when you are ready to admit it, the truth enters the innermost recesses of your being.

The conception of truth begins with love's unity.

In all areas of thought, we contradistinguish opposites to delineate opposing tendencies or extremes along a spectrum of experience—active and passive, positive and negative, forward and backward, action and reaction, future and past. Natural opposites are not always active and passive, or positive and negative in character and this is one difference between Equipoise and Taoist thought which always deals with an active and a passive (Yin and Yang). Equipoise can as equally well deal with a balance maintained between two active opposites. The balanced maintained need not be static but may be dynamic.

For any universal property, there is an antonym or opposite. Yet because these categories are obtained by dividing a continuum of experience into two groups, the totality of the all must include both equally. The nature of the all is, necessarily, that both or neither prevail overall. The nature of the all is best described by the interaction, balance, and unity of both.

This balance within a greater unity suggests that we should maintain a balance in our own endeavours, and experience teaches that extremes are best avoided. In dealing with a physical task, I might use too little strength or too much; the ideal is a midpoint between these extremes. In judgement of a social problem, we might use too much severity, which would be cruel, or too much tolerance, which would be negligent. In a matter of discernment we may be too indiscriminate, or too discriminating. By isolating extremes, we often lose track of the ideal midpoint, for which no adequate single word name exists, and yet this midpoint may be more often desirable than extremes in isolation. This is the excluded middle phenomenon whereby we have concepts for each opposite but no concept for their ideal balance.

Here my philosophy has entered a moral dimension and involves a value judgement that certain behaviour may be cruel by excessive severity or negligent by excessive tolerance. It is beginning to incorporate another distinction, between good and bad, right and wrong, based on metaphysics.

*   *   *

Good is the perfect balance of natural opposites.

Good and evil are not natural opposites; with clarity of thought, we should distinguish a balanced good from an imbalanced wrong, which might be of two kinds regarding a certain quality. We must learn to clearly differentiate between natural opposites and false dichotomies, which actually distinguish a balanced state from an imbalanced one. For example a man impelled by violent anger represents one extreme wrongdoing, and a man frozen by cowardice another opposite form of wrongdoing. How do we express the moderate and balanced Good of a man who will keep the peace if possible but resist bravely if necessary. Anger and fear represent an emotional spectrum in which a balance is preferable to either extreme.

Good is the nature of the whole and represented by the balance maintained within the whole.

Man is a natural being and culture an outgrowth of nature, through human nature. That good, or 'that which is of greater benefit', is in balance, in accordance with the anthropic condition. We require things to rest in the equilibrium they achieve in order to maintain life. (For example, if the earth were twenty degrees hotter or colder, we could not live in nature.) Natural systems exist in the balance of isotropic forces (*iso* meaning 'equal', *tropic* meaning 'place'). All phenomena exist in the balance of forces, such as the balance between gravity and rectilinear momentum (once called centrifugal force), which keeps planetary orbits stable (discovered by Newton). There is a metaphysical principle that requires and necessitates balance, a principle so universal it may be stated as a natural law.

*   *   *

The Law of Equipoise

Because ultimate reality is unitary, it is impossible that it resemble one natural opposite more than another; it must always resemble both, neither, or their balanced union. Because of this necessity, a natural law comes into operation.

The Law of Equipoise is the Law of Necessary balance and Necessary equivalence, which requires Necessary counterbalance.

The necessity of balance is entailed by the ultimate reality of unity.

Where a natural opposition exists, both implied opposites must equalise and combine within greater unity.

There is both necessary balance and necessary counterbalance to all extremes so that a balance prevails overall in a given system.

If balance is temporarily not maintained within that system, it will be equalised over time to create symmetry in a cyclic manner or counterbalanced within a larger encompassing system.

THE LAW OF EQUIPOISE APPLIES IN ALL SYSTEMS.

In rotary motion, it applies to the *paradox of the wheel*, in that any wheel in motion can be seen as spinning clockwise or anti-clockwise at the same rate from the perspective of each axis, though with a single motion. I have suggested this as a model for the cyclic nature of time which involves progressive and retrospective cycles equally though with an overall direction.

In the physics of motion, the limited statement of Equipoise is Newton's third law: For every action, there is an equal and opposite reaction.

In electrical theory the application of Equipoise is Kirchoff's law that the sum of all voltages, positive and negative, in an electrical system is zero; this proceeds from a more general law of the overall balance of charges (+ and -). In a DC circuit, the flows of charges may be viewed as electrons moving through space-time in one direction or in opposite counterbalance, positrons moving through space-time in the other direction (Feyman's QED).

In chemistry, Equipoise, the law of necessary balance, describes the balance of charges in stable atoms. A neutron contains the potential of a proton and an electron. The positive charges of protons and negative charges of electrons balance, except in ions (cations [+] and anions [-]). Atoms and molecules, when they acquire a change that brings them imbalance, combine with oppositely charged ions to form compounds in order to balance charge. This leads to chemical equilibrium. Chemical reactions are reversible, and proceeding in both directions, reach equilibrium in a given system, another application of Equipoise.

In biology Equipoise applies to the way natural organisms self-regulate to avoid extreme states, reaching the balance of *homeostasis*, a stable state. This is characteristic of all life forms and has led to the planetary organism hypothesis—the Gaia hypothesis of James Lovelock. Since the earth's natural systems also self-regulate to achieve balance. Equipoise may be taken further as a characteristic of God, the universal being.

In psychology, Equipoise applies to the balance and integration of a healthy mind, which does not take extreme states. It also applies to the counterbalancing extremes involved in abnormal psychological states, such as manic depression (high and low self-esteem, elation, and depression) or schizophrenia (fear/paranoia and anger/mania abreactions to threatening psycho-spiritual stimuli). Seen in terms of Equipoise, both are bipolar disorders occurring in counterbalancing extremes. Psychological balance is integral to a healthy mind. In interpersonal psychology, Equipoise involving necessary counterbalance explains what has been termed 'reverse psychology', fostering a tendency through its opposite assertion. However, this is not honest; but we must be wary of its accidental application and promote only a balanced view to avoid counterbalancing opposition.

In politics, Equipoise implies all extremities of government built on individualist social theory; seeing the individual as the primary cause and value in society (right wing) will be counteracted by holist influences, seeing society itself as the primary cause and value (left wing) and vice versa. Does the individual create society, or does society create the individual? Both views are valid, and must be synthesised and balanced. The extremes of right-wing and left-wing thinking cause necessary conflict between fascism and communism (Hitler's conflict with Stalin for instance). Their moderated balance, such as that found in our Australian political system, is almost ideal. Progressive and Retrospective (or conservative) influences must also achieve balance in an ideal political system according to Equipoise.

In relation to Justice, the concept of a necessary balance (Equipoise) is familiar. Because balance necessarily prevails overall, Natural Justice comes into operation, and our social systems of Justice seek to embody this balance through the adversarial system of prosecution and defence, which express and moderate severity and tolerance to arrive at a balanced outlook on the truth and justice of a given matter.

A moderated balance is preferable to a state of conflict between extremes. Moderated Equipoise, which contains and minimises opposites to avoid extremes, allowing for their creative conjunction, brings peace and harmony when embodied in society and in the world internationally. Equipoise is the most viable theory of peace studies and will be vital in the Lords' millennial rule of peace.

The Metaphysical Law and principle of Equipoise, is a profound truth that bears out empirical validation.

Many will say Equipoise is not new, but there is nothing else to notice other than that which is always and everywhere real and true.

'As Above so Below'

A system in microcosm can be equated with, or is analogous to, a system in macrocosm. Because Equipoise is the ruling principle in all systems, all systems are analogous, and they participate in greater unity.

Because the controlling balance of all natural systems is maintained within the ultimate reality—the unity of all in eternity through Equipoise—the nature of the soul and the selfhood of individual beings reflect the nature of the All in One and One in All, or God.

Natural and integral systems self-regulate to maintain balance. The nature of a response to a change in imbalance is a counterbalancing influence acting to re-establish balance, according to the natural Law of Equipoise, or necessary balance. A Human being is in the image of God through equipoise. In all ordered natural systems, a symmetry is apparent, reflecting the necessary balance in natural forms.

* * *

BEAUTY AND TRUTH ARE BOTH FORMS OF SYMMETRY— EQUIPOISE IN FORM

'"Beauty is truth, truth beauty"—that is all ye know on earth, and all ye need to know'

(John Keats, 'Ode on a Grecian Urn').

A statement of eternal truth is characteristically a statement of symmetry; any true equation states that one side is equal to the other. This is necessary equivalence. For example, the sum of the interior angles of a triangle is equal to two right angles; this is a statement of symmetry in equality, just as is $X=X$.

Our perception of beauty also rests in the perception of symmetry. The form of the human body displays bilateral symmetry. The beauty of a woman's two breasts perfectly matched, the balanced musculature of a man, or the radial symmetry of a flower—each are examples of beauty found in symmetry. Symmetry best conforms to the nature of ultimate reality, which expresses balance in unity. There is an ultimate standard, then, in both truth and beauty, which lies in its perfect resemblance to equivalent balance. However, asymmetries, in contrast to symmetry, may provide a contrast contraindicating the ideal

GOD IS GOOD.

The being which includes all being, the awareness which includes all awareness, maintains the natural balance of equipoise. Existing in the totality of all, unity in eternity, God's character cannot be represented partially. God is in all things but is not equivalent to any section or portion of these things. God maintains the natural overall balance; God is good. That is, God is represented by the perfect balance of natural opposites, the true good. The balance best represents the character of the All in One. Good and evil have been traditionally conceived of as opposites; they are not natural opposites but form a distinction between a naturally balanced and an imbalanced state.

MORALITY BUILT ON EQUIPOISE METAPHYSICS

Because love in principle unites opposites, homosexuality and particularly Sodomy (named from the city the angels destroyed) is a vice and a crime against nature. Its opposite extremity in imbalance, however, is homophobic prejudice, which sees two males or females embracing slandered unreasonably, as if homosexual. This is the inevitable conclusion of a morality built on Equipoise metaphysics. It is the practice not the person we should condemn as all are equals.

Innocence must be protected and paedophilia is an offense against the essential nature of the child self not yet matured into full sexual differentiation. Its opposite imbalance, however, is unreasonable suspicion and blame attached to non-ageist love relationships that are not even physically sexual. A girl old enough to bear children is not a child, but a young woman, and there is no reason the New Age should be more intolerant than the Victorian era with respect to either natural man and maiden unions or 'cougar' unions. An extreme abreaction has taken place during the millennial transition to the airing of the paedophilia issue in that is seems society is so out of balance it would be more acceptable for a 40 year old man to have a homosexual partner than to have a teenage sweetheart of the opposite sex. The issue runs contrary to anti-ageism as we are all equals of any age

Extreme social tolerance has abreacted into 'zero tolerance' policies; and zero tolerance into extreme tolerance. Sodomy was once a criminal offense in many countries but we now see it promoted as a form of 'marriage'. The ideal balance must be reached to prevent further Equipoise alteration.

There are two possible imbalances that exist in counterbalance on either side of the balanced good. Good is necessary, where evil is not. Evil is imbalance, error, and the result of beings of limited awareness having freedom and being unreconciled to being in God.

The applied metaphysics of Equipoise provides the final key to the overcoming of evil as unnecessary and, so, best dispensed with.

THE DOCTRINE OF NECESSARY EQUALITY

We are all necessary equals within the necessary Unity of all in Eternity, God. Each of us with the Logos mind of God within. Each of us in the Nature of God. Each of us Elohim, Children of God, actual or potential Angels of light. Each of us maintaining within the necessary balance of *Equipoise*, which is the innermost balance of nature, the prevailing Way in all the world, and the making and shaping of all events.

This doctrine sums up changes in effect in the transition of the ages and provides a metaphysical basis for Human Rights in every country. So welcome to the new Age where all men, women, and children all over the world shall live as equals, and equals to the angels (because all are potential angels).

As this doctrine takes hold in the mind of God, the minds of angel *Elohim*, and unconsciously in the minds of all humankind we see tyrannical systems all over the world challenged and falling. Racism, Sexism, and Ageism are in steady decline as are all hierarchies of inequity. Ageism which used to enslave children ('shut up, sit down, do what your told') and excludes the elderly, preventing cross generational mixing is the newest forefront of moral advance.

There is still need for further change toward human rights of equality. Despite tyrannical regimes across the Arab world being challenged by spontaneous uprisings as in Egypt, Syria, and Libya, Australia for one country cannot afford to point a finger at human rights violators abroad. Not while it still has States such as Western Australia whose Police Act State Law recognizes no human rights and allows for daily and systematic human rights violations particularly toward Aboriginal People. They are caught in a conflict of Law and Culture penalized for their Law based right and duty to take the Law into their own hands and subject to Human rights abuse by Police and the Prison system. A developed Australian Common Law which acknowledges underlying Aboriginal Law and given additional Human Rights protection made regular in all the States would be the best solution.

Chapter 19

EQUIPOISE SYMBOLS AND THE UNIFIED EVENT

Principles are patterns inherent in nature, in the order implicit.

The Equipoise symbol diagram and its derived symbols, which are found within the main key symbol diagram, are more than models, or arbitrary symbols standing for words. They are principles and patterns of implicit order. Though mathematics deals with eternal numbers. Equipoise principle patterns are also eternal forms in the Logos mind of God and can furnish predictions and understandings directly, without maths or verbal interpretation.

Taken with the attendant Equipoise metaphysical philosophy of necessary balance, equivalence, and counterbalance within the ultimate reality of the unity of all in all space-time—Equipoise Principle Patterns can describe the implicit relation of forces in a unified event.

Taking our familiar planet Earth as the basis of a more universal understanding, we can apply the Equipoise principle patterns to an understanding of the unified event of a spinning globe in space-time.

Figure 19.1 The Key Equipoise Principle Pattern applied to the Earths Globe

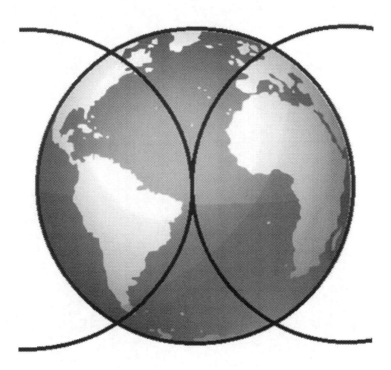

We see that the central axis of symmetry in the diagram can be aligned naturally with the earth's axis of rotation, which runs from pole to pole. The earth spins clockwise in relation to its south pole and anti-clockwise in relation to its north pole. The length of a day is the time taken for the earth to revolve once, and a year is the time taken for the earth to complete an orbit of the Sun.

The implicit relationship between time and space is inherent in this relationship of axial rotation. Time is intrinsically linked to cyclic rotation in space, which can be viewed as either clockwise or anti-clockwise, dependant on perspective. These apparent opposites unified in one motion.

* * *

The first derived symbol is the dipole, or magnetic principle, which describes the magnetic force aligned with the earth's axis of rotation. A monopole is not possible in nature. Electron Spin and the earth's rotation regularise the alignment of the individual fields of atoms and electrons into a coherent dipolar magnetic alignment.

19.2 The Dipole or Magnetic Principle Pattern

We may divide a dipole into north and south poles, as we conventionally do with magnets, as well as with the earth. Yet these apparent opposites are unified in equivalence, and the field alignment is regular throughout the axis, not at any point reversed. The field strength of north and south poles must always be equal, which is an application of the law of Equipoise. The magnetic field joins the poles in an array of arcs.

*   *   *

The second derived symbol is the 'grav', or gravitic principle.

Figure 19.3 The 'Grav' or Principle Pattern of Gravity

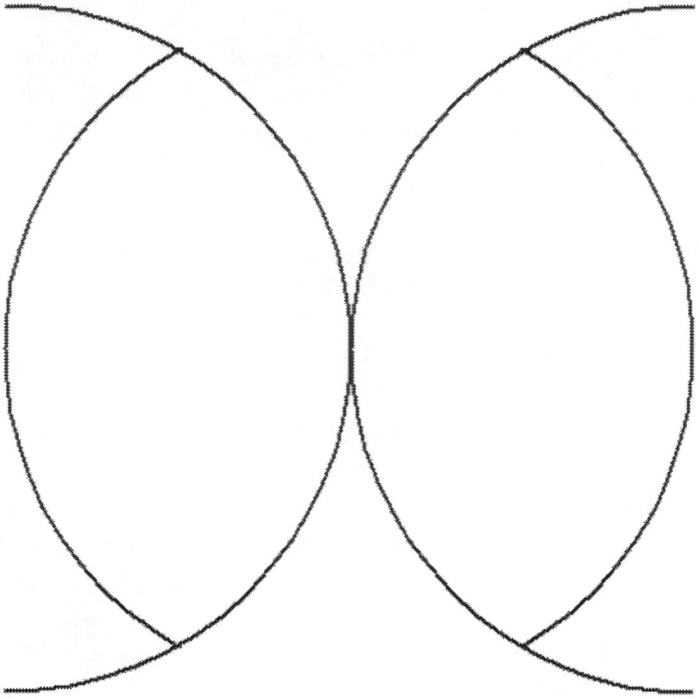

All the planets orbit the sun in the same regular plane of orbit (making the solar system disk shaped) like the moon's orbit of the earth; this is approximately perpendicular to the planetary axis of rotation and magnetic axis. The sun contains 99.9 per cent of the mass of the whole solar system, so the solar system's centre of mass is within it.

Why the solar system should be disk shaped is not accounted for by either Newton's or Einstein's theory of gravitation. It may be stated as derived from the first principles of equipoise, that the primary gravitational plane runs perpendicular to the planetary and solar axis. (This is clearly shown in planets, such as Saturn, forming equatorial rings.) Observed departure from the ideal (the earth is offset around 23 degrees, causing the seasons) must have come from the application of a force at some stage. Possibly this was the earth catching its moon, which stabilises its new alignment.

The geometry of the form allows for up to 30 degrees departure from the perpendicular as an axis is not defined.

We see from the symbol that the axis becomes excluded from the rotation of mass effect. What we have, in essence, is a unifying force within the planet, which is delocalised in space-time according to the inverse square law as a force of attraction.

As indicated by the 'grav', this is primarily in a plane at right angles to the magnetic axis of rotation (by imaginary extension of the line endings in a straight line). Due to the gravitic principle, the mass of the planet is unified in equivalence as a sphere.

Any geocentric explanation of gravity would ignore the gravito/magnetic plane of the sun, which has 99.9 per cent of all the solar system's mass with proportionally greater gravity (and its spin axis only 7 degrees from perpendicular to its gravitic plane in our neat disk-shaped system). The principle patterns can also be applied to the Sun, any planet, or any Star.

The recently discovered 'tenth planet', Sedna, is likely a newcomer caught in oblique transit orbit and should not yet be considered a planet. However, Equipoise predicts that it will settle into the sun's gravitic plane and become one eventually.

*   *   *

The third derived symbol is the 'electro', or electric principle pattern which describes the relation of electric force to the spinning magnetic-gravitational body of mass. Its image depicts waveform materially contained.

Figure 19.4 The 'Electro' or Principle Pattern of Electricity—Progressive form

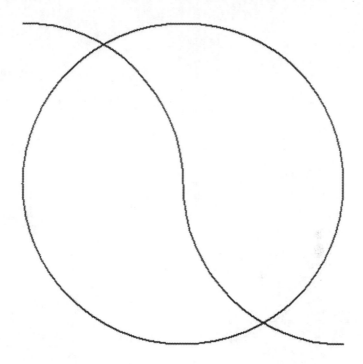

A conducting disk or sphere spun in an axial magnetic field alignment generates charge separation. In this way, electricity generation was discovered, through the Faraday disk dynamo experiment. If the axial magnetic field results from regular axial magnets fixed on the disk or sphere, rotating with it, the effect still occurs (dubbed the 'N' effect by Physicist Bruce De Palma) as it does in the planet.

The low voltage separation of charge caused by rotation in an axially aligned magnetic field is subject to electrical condensation through atmospheric capacitance. This causes the high voltage discharge we experience as lightning. This symbol is envisaged as aligned in the perpendicular plane to the axis (like a slice through the earth's equator). It suggests rotation by its cyclic form and can be shown in two forms, progressive and retrospective (clockwise and anti-clockwise) though these are different perspectives on the same motion.

Figure 19.5 The 'Electro' or Principle Pattern of Electricity—Retrospective form

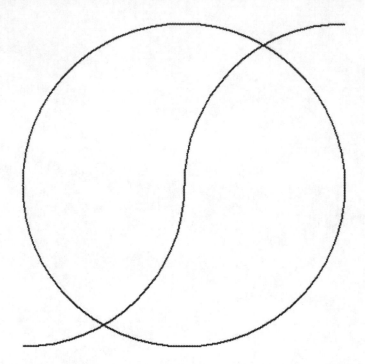

Electric charge displacement can be viewed as a flow of negative electrons in one direction or positive positrons in the other. Richard Feynman, the founder of quantum electrodynamics, says a positron can be regarded as an electron moving backward in time. Electric current flows in order to re-establish charge equivalence in accordance with the law of Equipoise. This principle pattern gives an image of the positron on a retrospective cycle (future to past) as distinct from the electron on a progressive cycle (past to future).

*   *   *

The next derived symbol is the 'Wav' describing the electromagnetic waveform of light in photon form as a wave packet, which has been released from material containment in the electron. This also has two possible forms; these are most likely the two waveforms of light involved in natural unpolarised light, where polarised light has only one of these waveforms.

Figure 19.6 The 'Wav', Photon, or wave packet Principle Pattern of Light—Progressive form

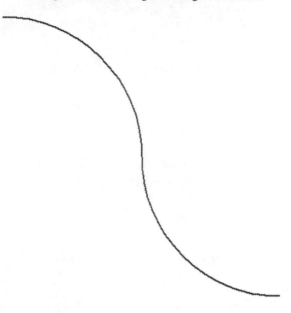

Figure 19.7 The 'Wav', Photon, or wave packet Principle Pattern of Light—Retrospective form

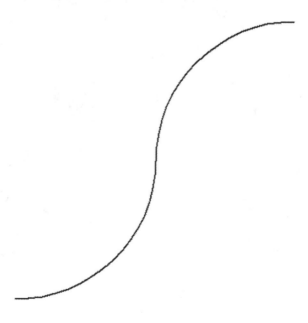

* * *

$$E = Mc^2$$

To satisfy Equipoise, this reduces to E=M. Where E = Energy, and M = Mass of Matter. This is enabled by defining light speed (c) as one 'lux' (one light year per year), whereupon one squared drops out of the equation and the units for mass and energy are adjusted to make universal light relative natural units. If it is possible for light relative interrelation of units the equation is no longer based on arbitrary measures such as the length of a standard platinum bar in a Paris museum (the Metre). Light relativity is still conveyed by the wav or photon forms which unite and equalise Energy and Matter.

Figure 19.8 Equipoise Equivalent Balance of Energy and Matter

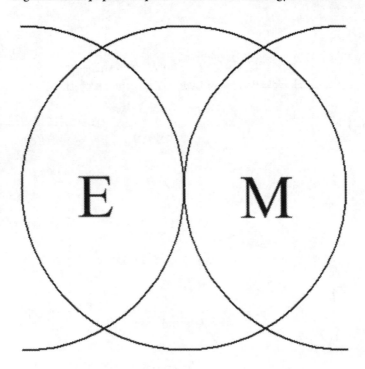

* * *

Nuclear forces and Nuclear—genesis.

Figure 19.9 Equipoise Depiction of the Hydrogen Atom—Proton and Electron

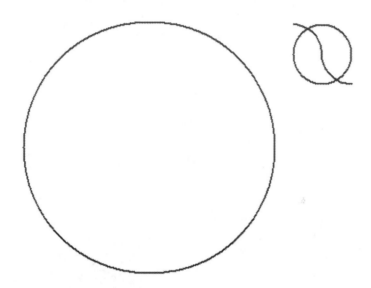

The above diagram depicts the simplest of all atoms, hydrogen. It has a nucleus composed of a single proton, which is orbited by a single electron. The electron (-) is shown with the equipoise electric principle pattern, which describes how it can potentially absorb or emit electromagnetic waveform energy as photons (photo-electric excitation or incandescence). The simple circle represents the virgin proton (+) (uninvolved in nuclear bonding) as a sphere in this picture.

In the basic components of the hydrogen atom, we may have all we need to make any and all atoms through stellar fusion. However, the next step is creating a neutron, which happens when a proton absorbs an electron and contains it in an internal, not external, orbit. The resultant particle, the neutron, is electrically neutral. The neutron, alternatively, may be viewed as the more primal and as the source of protons and electrons, as a free neutron can produce a proton and an electron.

Figure 19.10 Principle Pattern of the Strong Nuclear Force & Helium atomic Nucleus

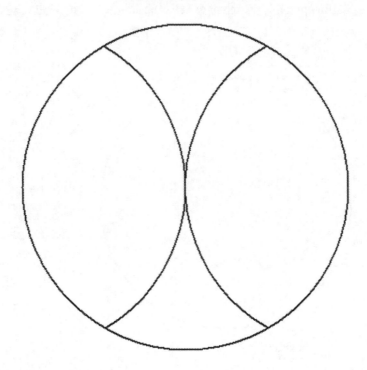

The principle pattern above gives a picture of the strongest of all forces—the strong nuclear force that binds the atomic nucleus together, a force of integrity. It represents two protons (as mandorla saucers) that are compressed by this force and bonded by a central neutron. To visualise this in three dimensions, think of a sphere containing two hemispherical zones meeting centrally. The neutron form is a platelet shape with concave faces containing an electron in internal orbit. The beauty of this arrangement is the complementarity of the two forms. With every extra neutron added, you can stack an extra proton (and electron), leading to heavier and heavier elements. This is the divine alchemy of fusion, which creates elements in the hearts of stars, like our sun. The principle pattern may be placed on either the earth or the Sun and stars.

This leads to the theory that heavier elements are produced by fusion reactions in the cores of planets like our Earth. The secondary Geo-fusion hypothesis. Lead and Gold have not conceivably escaped the gravity of the

Sun or Stars and floated through empty space to arrive on earth. The earth's core is as hot as the surface temperature of the Sun (around 5,500 C). This would not be possible if gravity were the only source of heat. A fusion reaction is heating the earth's core. Also our Sun is not known to contain these elements. Alluvial gold arises from the earth's core where it is formed beneath the molten iron level.

Here may lie the truth of the Alchemical maxim—'VITRIOL': *"Visita Interiora Terrae Rectificando Invenies Occultum Lapidem.* Which Translates "Visit the Interior Parts of the Earth; by Rectification Thou Shalt Find the Hidden Stone." That is the *Philosophers Stone* responsible for transmutation of the elements.

The weak nuclear force comes into operation mostly in heavy atoms and involves neutrons, or protons in beta decay, and is the resultant force of all forces to disintegrity.

Figure 19.11 The 'Darkon' or Principle Pattern of Weak Nuclear Force

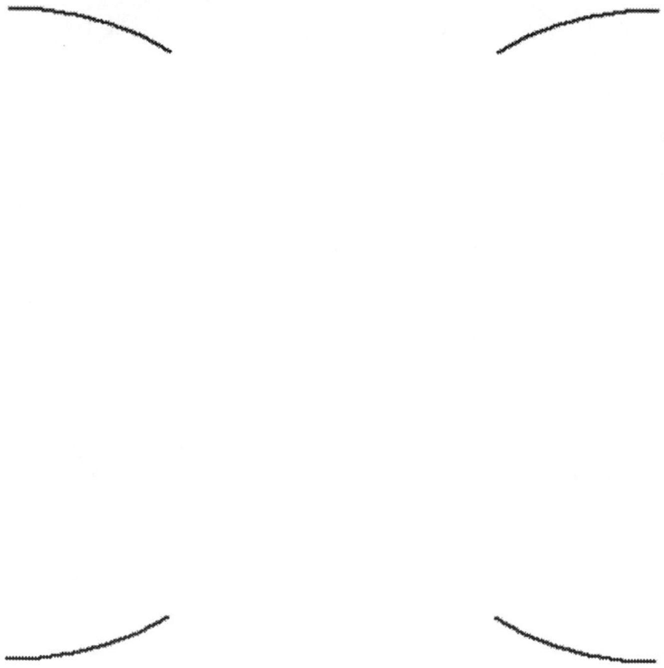

The above symbol is the 'Darkon' or principle Pattern of weak nuclear force. Its lines may also be equated with gamma radiation (light of short wavelength) and its opposite waveform. It has a cosmic equivalent in the expansive force that opposes gravity 'Dark energy'.

* * *

'Chronos'[5] is the principle pattern of time that describes a spinning body of mass and the inextricably associated phenomenon of time. It can be shown in progressive and retrospective forms, which are the two perceived directions in cyclic time, though they are united and differ only in perspective. Chronos progressive is the forward cycle of time from past to future. All things and all beings are involved in cyclic repetition in time-space governed by Logos and Equipoise (necessary balance) in retrospective and progressive cycles equally.

Figure 19.12 Chronos Progressive Cycle, the forward Principle Pattern of Time

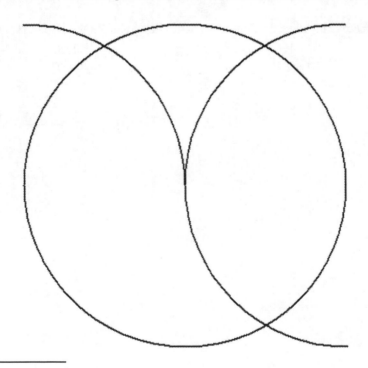

---

5   I am using the word 'Chronos' as a coined word to describe the principle pattern of Time, not the Greek personification of time. I have tried to coin words so the principle patterns can be referred to in shorthand

Figure 19.13 Chronos Retrospective Cycle, the reverse Principle Pattern of Time

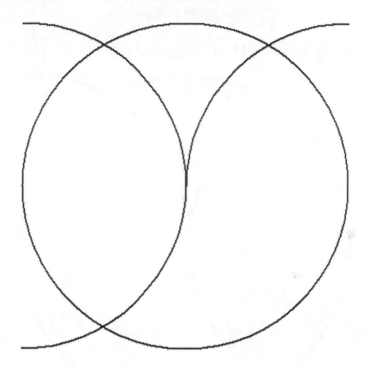

Chronos shows the three dimensions of space involved in Cyclic Time—the fourth dimension.

Equipoise is a Metaphysical system of principles as patterns—universal forms in the ordering mind of Logos.

The lines outside the circle or sphere in the Equipoise Key Principle Pattern have no real existence in substance; they are purely lines of force. For this reason, time itself, having three external force lines in the Chronos form, is, in equipoise metaphysics, regarded as a force. Indeed, it is the force that shapes the universe through time paradox, making and shaping all things. Strong nuclear force, in contrast, has only internal force lines and weak nuclear force, no internal force lines.

Figure 19.14 The Key Equipoise Principle Pattern applied to the Spherical Model of Space-time

Future End of space-time: Omega Event

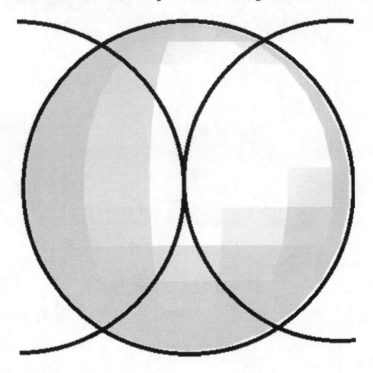

Past Beginning of space-time Alpha Event

Applying the Equipoise Key Principal Pattern to the spherical model of space-time (a standard model), we can see how the universe has expanded from the 'big bang', or alpha event (bottom of diagram), until gravity overtakes the force of the original explosion and expansion (equatorial point). This leads to the 'big crunch', or Omega event (top of diagram), which will end all space-time. These are actually one unified event having no space or time to separate them, either prior to or after all space-time. Our God in greater unity exists as unified singularity, the alpha and omega, the first and the last. Within space-time the alpha and omega event is connected by the axis of the mid-heavens. If the penultimate spiritual 'heaven' has a location in space-time it is central to the entire universe. Our earth, indeed, must be very near the axis of the mid-heavens at this time, as it appears most stars proceed away from us with the earth being central.

'I am the Alpha and the Omega, The Beginning and the End, the First and the Last.' (Revelation 22:13)

Chapter 20

EQUIPOISE IN THE ETERNAL DREAMING

My EQUIPOISE SYMBOL, although not passed on to me from an Aboriginal source (but coming from a dream) was I believe Aboriginal at one stage and can be used to illustrate and explain Aboriginal Dreamings (Dreamtime Stories and Law) from Minyirr, located in Broome West Australia, where I worked as an anthropologist and as a shaman for 15 years. Much of this information is traditional Aboriginal Law & culture passed on to me by Elders now deceased, some from my shamanic spiritual experience. I asked my son Laib for his permission to publish them since he was initiated at Minyirr and this is his legitimate cultural right among the Minyurrjuno (belonging to Minyirr) Yawuru people. This is Minyirr Buggarigarra (Minyirr Law of The Eternal Dreaming).

The Dreaming of the Ganananga and the First Aboriginal Ancestors, Didir and Jukakon

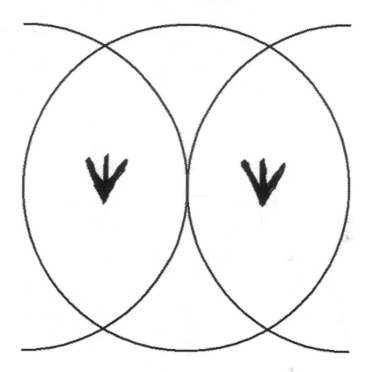

In the Eternal Dreaming, the first man and first woman emerged from the sea at Minyirr in Broome. Their names were Didir and Jukakon. They united in Love and gave birth to the first family of Australian ancestors. At a certain stage, a *ganananga* came along past Minyirr point. The *ganananga* is a creature of mystery, who left distinctive three toed footprints on the alluvial rock at Gantheaume point, as did the first ancestral family leave human footprints. The old man, with his *yila* (dingo ancestors) first fought with the *ganananga*, but it was very powerful and fought them to a standoff. They established the law of mutual respect, or Goodyera Gurriji (respect between the two) and reconciled.

Gudeya (white) people say the one who left the three-toed footprints was a dinosaur; some aboriginal people think it emu-like or an emu-man (there are various versions), but it may have been more like a winged dinosaur or dragon. You can find out for yourself what it was by sitting in the rock shelter at the point overnight and singing, '*Jalangu inambarum, jalangu inambarum,*

Minyirr *bugarrigara'*. (Rough translation—To shamanise, in the first law of Minyirr in the eternal dreaming.)

Goodyera Gurriji became the first law of Australia and the basis for all future law in society. As the Aboriginal people spread out across the continent, they took this first law with them wherever they went. Apart from respect, *gurriji* can also mean 'awe of the sacred.' The Law of mutual respect is in accord with the law of equipoise or 'necessary equality' and also with the law of Christ—'Do unto others as you would have them do unto you.'

The Goodyera Jurru (The Two Snakes)

In the dreaming, a male snake called Olgadon lived at Minyirr, and a female snake called Jabirr from Jabirr-Jabirr country in the north (where the women held the law and were like an Amazon tribe) swam down to meet the male. The two at first fought over territory but later reconciled according to the law of Goodyera Gurriji already laid down there. They mated, and the female snake surrendered her powers to the male snake, which made it then 'the Rainbow Serpent' and the most powerful of all the giant serpents of the eternal dreaming.

Loom and the First Fire

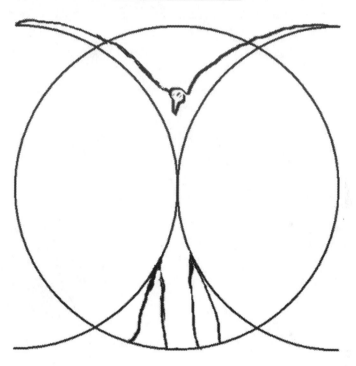

From Jabirr-Jabirr country to the North comes the story of the first fire. A mixed group of Jabirr-Jabirr and Nyull-Nyull peoples would fish together in the clear blue waters of the Dampier Peninsula. A stranger, the old man Loom came along with them day after day to spearfish with them but would always take his catch off and not eat with the other people. One day, two *malarr* (young women) got curious about him and followed him down south as he crossed two creeks to where his camp was, at Loomaburr (the place of Loom). Here they found him sitting by a campfire, cooking his fish. The two girls had never seen a fire before.

Up until that time, fire had been one man's secret, and Loom was put wrong by revealing his sacred secret. He transformed into his totem animal, the fire hawk, or *Jungu billbill*, and rose above the flames. The girls ran in and carried off fire sticks and took them back to their people. Later, they returned to become Loom's wives. They can be seen in the picture as the two womanly vulva shapes as their *jindis* were open before him. Even today, the fire hawk can be seen following the front of bushfires and swooping on the small animals it flushes out. It is as if it carries the fire front with it.

The Goodyera Wati (Two Man) Dreaming

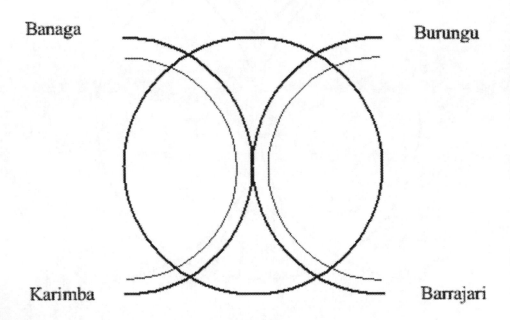

Banaga

Burungu

Karimba

Barrajari

In the Dreaming, two men ancestral culture heroes travelled from inland all over the Western desert and returned the Law to Minyirr. They were the first men to be circumcised, as they circumcised each other becoming the first *yalburu* (brothers-of-law). They introduced this law into aboriginal initiation ceremonies. The *nurlu* (song) they left is chanted to two *irragal* (boomerangs) clapped together.

If you look at the equipoise symbol, you can make out two circumcised *banja* (penises) meeting in the middle. You can make out boomerang shapes back to back (as they are used for percussion) in the middle of the symbol

The Two ancestral men also gave the law of the four skin-groups and told people which skin group they were and who it was right and wrong to marry. The law of the four skin groups told people to relate to everyone in society in mutual respect relationships and was built on the first law of Minyirr. It can be read as a skin group diagram—Banaga marries Burungu; Karimba marries Barrajari. The path of the snake connects father to offspring, and the woman's path (a curve) connects mother to offspring.

There may be a natural and genetic truth in skin-groups law as it predicts similarity between grandchildren and either mothers mother, or fathers father. You could arrive at this by gene pairing AA marries BB . . . offspring are AB or BA (depending on sex linked dominance) only through mating of AB and BA do we arrive again at pure AA and BB (depending on sex linked dominance).

The Goodyera Wati is the Australian equivalent of the Covenant of Abraham as it makes circumcision a sacred duty, in this case a rite of transition to manhood.

Chapter 21

IN SPIRIT AND IN TRUTH

JESUS HIMSELF TAUGHT, in John 4:24, 'God is Spirit (pneuma), and those who worship him must worship in spirit and in truth.' Pneuma is the original Greek for spirit. However, this need not mean God is spirit only, as traditional theism commonly conceives (or spirit only, excepting when, as Christ, the word—Logos—became flesh). But it is, nonetheless, intrinsic to the Christian concept of God that God is, in a primary sense, spirit.

Angels, too, are spirits, as this passage indicates: 'And of the angels He says: Who makes His angels spirits' (Hebrews 1:7). (Pneuma means spirit, or breath of breeze). This is a New testament quote of an old testament verse originally from Psalm 104:4, where the Hebrew *ruwach* also means spirit, breath, or air, though associated with qualities of mind.

Let us, then, consider the nature of spirit. The Greek word *pneuma* relates in its root meaning to a movement of air, breath, or breeze. This might relate to the concept of an invisible fluid. Metaphysical philosophy and theology have contributed to the meaning of *spirit*. The 'rational spirit' imbues it with qualities of mind. 'Essence'—the essential quality of a thing abstracted from the thing itself—was equated with spirit. 'The efficient cause of motivation' became a conception of spirit, drawing on metaphysics of causation for explanation. In more recent popular psychology usage, 'spirit' is just an emotional quality in the individual mind and shared by groups.

Going back to the root meaning of 'breath' or 'breeze', this idea of spirit may relate to the basic observations of a shaman.

I want to add the observation that spirits, including angels, readily interact with air, so that a spirit presence may be felt as a breeze and spirit voices can speak with an equivalent of breath. The confirmation, or otherwise, of this observation must rest in the reader's own experience. For me though, it is an additional mystery that I require explained by a full metaphysical account of the nature of spirit.

In this age, where so many invisible phenomena, such as magnetic, electric, and gravitational fields, are the subject of attempted explanation in physics, the metaphysician should be able to similarly tackle a rational account of spirit.

In reaching my conclusions as to the nature of spirit, I have been guided by a premise that has been fruitful of many insights—*the ultimate reality is unity of all in eternity: God.*

Unlike mystics—who have arrived at this point and stopped there, considering ultimate reality ineffable and concepts dividing it to be fundamentally flawed—I have found it possible to reason from this premise and reach true conclusions, as one might in considering whether energy and matter, or time and space, are ultimately separable. A meta-logic of unitary ultimate reality where unity is held primary and conceptual division secondary.

Consider, then, The Ultimate reality, unchanging, eternal, and all-encompassing. Within this eternal unity is contained the transient reality of each passing moment. The everyday reality of 'the present' is not separate, then, from the eternal unity of God but contained within it. The reality of being in this time and all other times are included within eternal unity.

Spirit, then, is the category of existence of being that may not be physically enduring in the present but maintains an apparent endurance, as it exists always within eternal unity. Another way of expressing this is to say that the reality of beings in the present is not separable from that of beings at any and all other times, and this is sensed as what we call 'spirit'.

There is another characteristic of spirit apart from apparent endurance that my key premise helps us approach. In the reality of the present moment, living beings appear separate, yet the ultimate reality (God) is a unity inclusive of them. Spirit, then, can be seen as intermediate to the ultimate reality of unity, unifying individuals and connecting them in the greater being of God. It enables communication in spirit.

The ability of spirit to unify individuals is also noted in scripture: 'Endeavouring to keep the unity of the Spirit in the bond of peace. There is one body and one Spirit ... One God and Father of all, who is above all, and through all, and in you all' (Ephesians 4: 3-5).

Love is a unifying principle, and spirit a unifying medium. Thus, God is Love, and God is Spirit, for *God is the ultimate reality of unity in eternity.*

Spirit, then, is not a category of substance but an aspect of the eternal, all-embracing ultimate reality as it appears at all times. Its nature is more readily explicable in terms of time, the reality of the present being secondary to the ultimate reality of the eternal, the unity of all, in all space-time.

However, if we consider the apparent opposites, spirit and substance, we must conclude from the stated premise that they cannot have freestanding separable existence. Spirit cannot manifest in the absence of substance and, perhaps, cannot exist entirely in the absence of substance. My conclusion, then, is that spirit is not an invisible fluid (like air), but its manifestation is dependent on the presence of some substance and more readily noticeable when interacting with a fluid, gaseous medium such as air. Water may act as an insulating barrier to all but pure spirit, and fire, such as in the molten inner earth, as a purifying agent. The interaction of spirit and substance, though, is not presently well understood.

I still struggle to understand what it is fire purifies spirit of, and how, though I believe it does and as a Seraph Elohim it is one of my gifts.

God, then, is inclusive of all spirit and is the universal and eternal spirit, within which is the Godhead, which accesses all awareness at all times and exemplifies Logos, the divine intelligence. Spirit is not ultimately separable from mind, and the medium of spirit is impressed by mind and unites minds. Yet the confluence or merging of minds and beings can take place within space-time in a number of ways. It is, primarily, guided by love as a unifying principle and felt in the desire to unify.

The angelic spirits' awareness is divine awareness of being in God through love. We need not consider how many angels may fit on the head of a pin (an argument that concerns whether angels occupy space), but I do have a real question and concern about whether there can truly be 'many angels' as distinct beings.

To my mode of thinking, angels—being closer to the presence of the Godhead and sharing, in some degree, in God's eternal awareness—must have limited or qualified individuality, and my spiritual experience confirms this. They are Elohim, or beings in God. In their angelic spiritual nature, they approach, the eternal unity of being in God with the consequent loss of transient separateness. Angels merge in unhampered loving spiritual union with each other and with the Lord God.

It is the imprint of Logos, divine ordering intelligence, that gives spirit its integrity and separateness as souls. Logos is the gift of consciousness itself and the ability to self-reflect. Yet, Logos is the divine intelligence of spirit and cannot impede its unity with the Godhead.

Taking a broader world view, we can understand how spirit has so many manifestations and different spiritual beings have been known in different cultures and times by the capability of spirit to mix and unify in different ways, which I term 'spiritual confluence.' The man-animal hybrids of native religion and shamanism may be seen as the products of spiritual confluence, though they are not ultimately real, or real for all time. I have found shamanism vital to understanding Satan as a serpent-man confluence hybrid who influences people to strike without thinking, and Lucifer's lineage of egotistic pseudo angels as dragon-man confluence hybrids descended from Marduk the dragon slayer god of Babylon.

Lower animals, though they have spirit, have no individual souls and merge in a species spirit. They do not have the imprint of Logos, or not to the same degree, which gives conceptual awareness and the ability to self-reflect. This enables subjective 'I' selfhood formation in humans.

Spirits who are unreconciled to being in God are the cause of many spiritual problems for living beings, for we mix in spirit with a number of temporal spiritual hybrids, while retaining our separate subjective Logos souls. The soul does not enclose us fully in spirit, but rather, centres us. *Confluence*, the mixing of spirits, and *Concordance*, the unity of accord, are two factors in determining everyday spiritual influences.

It is interesting to look in scripture at examples of the shamanism of Jesus. Understand, I am not trying to characterise Jesus as simply a Shaman, but since he worked with spirits for a healing purpose, we may fairly say that he was a Shaman (just as we might describe him fairly as a public speaker or teacher, without implying that was all he was).

Any Christian who believes the gospel record must believe in spirits who may cause madness and sickness, as there are many examples of Jesus and his apostles treating people affected by such spirits. However, Christ and the apostles did more than dispel harmful spirits; they also imbued people with the Holy Spirit, which could affect instantaneous cures, reordering damaged flesh to give sight to the blind and healthy limbs to the lame. The Holy Spirit, then, carries the perfect ordering intelligence of Logos, which includes the perfect form of the body.

The strange testimony of spirits is a theme that runs through the gospels. Spirits often recognise Jesus as the Son of God and cause people to cry out in that manner, whereupon he dispels them. This has always struck me as odd. In a way, these spirits appear to be those of pious Christians.

I can imagine a type of Christian (though one who does not understand the mystery of his or her faith) whose most fervent wish was to meet Jesus in person; this person suddenly finds that he or she has spiritual mobility in space and time and is able to see Jesus in person through the eyes of a contemporary spectator. If anything makes such a spirit 'evil', it must be because it invades or possesses a living person and is not reconciled to being in God, perhaps due to limited awareness and guilt, or the burden of sin.

Consider the following passage: 'Now in the synagogue there was a man who had a spirit of an unclean demon. And he cried out with a loud voice, saying, "Let us alone! What have we to do with You, Jesus of Nazareth?

Did You come to destroy us? I know who You are-the Holy One of God!"
But Jesus rebuked him, saying, "Be quiet, and come out of him!"' (Luke 4:
33-35).

To speak, though, of individual spirits can be misleading, since they are
often involved in spiritual confluence, mixing with other spirits, which can
make them impure or unclean.

This is one of the themes indicated by the incident with the possessed man
at the tombs:

> When he saw Jesus, he cried out, fell down before Him, and with
> a loud voice said, 'What have I to do with You, Jesus, Son of the
> Most High God? I beg You, do not torment me!' For He had
> commanded the unclean spirit to come out of the man. For it had
> often seized him, and he was kept under guard, bound with chains
> and shackles; and he broke the bonds and was driven by the demon
> into the wilderness. Jesus asked him, saying, 'What is your name?'
> And he said, 'Legion,' because many demons had entered him. And
> they begged Him that He would not command them to go out
> into the abyss. Now a herd of many swine was feeding there on
> the mountain. So they begged Him that He would permit them to
> enter them. And He permitted them. Then the demons went out of
> the man and entered the swine, and the herd ran violently down the
> steep place into the lake and drowned. (Luke 8:28-33)

The unfortunate man was possessed by a confluence of spirits, too many
to name, so he called them 'legion'. Note, though, that although Jesus cured
the man of his possession, he allowed the spirits (perhaps because some
recognised him) liberty. Though the man was cured, what happened to the
spirits when the swine died? They cannot have been destroyed along with
the pigs. Perhaps, though, the confluence was dispersed.

Simply casting out spirits is not a complete solution to spiritual ills. Cast out
of one house or person, they may enter the next. They might be suppressed
below the earth to purify, or bound to the pit (earth's core), but this may
be peremptory of the final judgement and may not always be effective.

Take authority, though, when dealing with spirits, as Jesus taught, for you represent God. Spirits are not wiser than we are.

The solution to eternal spirits being unreconciled to being in God and leading living persons astray could not be an overnight one; a growth of awareness in spiritual reconciliation, and spiritual cleansing by the baptism of water and of fire must play a part, and in last resort, containment, which happens on the authority of the Godhead. Even the most powerful of adversarial spirits can be described as fallen angels. We read, 'Now all things are of God, who has reconciled us to Himself through Jesus Christ, and has given us the ministry of reconciliation, that is, that God was in Christ reconciling the world to Himself, not imputing their trespasses to them, and has committed to us the word of reconciliation' (2 Corinthians 5:18).

What does it mean to worship God in Sprit and in truth ? To worship God in spirit is clear and conventional enough, through prayer and other devotions. To worship God in truth is, in essence, approaching awareness of God through divine metaphysics. What, then, characterises Christ's metaphysics?

Though Christ was conventional enough to quote the Torah in his teachings, he brought a new focus to Love as the basis of Law We read Christ's teaching in Mark 12:30 "And You Shall Love the Lord your God with all your heart, with all your soul, with all your mind and with all your strength" This is the first commandment '.(This verse Christ quoted from Deuteronomy 6:4,5) And in the next verse Christ says ; Mark 12: 31 "And the second like it is this : 'You shall love your neighbour as yourself' (This Verse Christ quotes from Leviticus 19:18)

In all his teachings, Christ Yeshua emphasised a new aspect of the eternal Way :

Inner = outer Equipoise
Love of self = love of neighbours
Self-respect = respect of others

'Judge not lest you be judged'—judgement of others = judgement received

A necessary inner = outer, balance of equivalence

Understood correctly, "Do Unto others, as you would have them do unto you" is not merely a moral dictum but a statement of natural and metaphysical Law which might be restated 'As ye do unto others, so shall it be done unto you'. It is as invariable as the laws of physics—a statement of Equipoise or necessary equivalence, just as in 'for every action there is an equal and opposite reaction'. Metaphysics and universals must necessarily be the basis for moral law, for if not, it would be the purely artificial product of human culture.

Chapter 22

THE PSYCHO-SPIRITUAL

In the mid to late 1800s in Germany, a new manner of looking at the human psyche and mind was emerging from scientific study. The word *psyche* is the Greek word for 'soul'. Psychology became the scientific study of the human mind and soul, or essential selfhood, shedding all religious and spiritual notions in this study.

Sigmund Freud, along with Bruke, a physiologist who was his lecturer, Herman von Helmholtz (a physicist), Ludwig, and Bois-Reymond formed a kind of private society. They agreed that no other forces were operative within the individual organism apart from the purely physical and chemical ones. In psychology this was a revolution against spiritual explanations based on Christianity.

Freud, the founder of psychoanalysis, used the energetic model of the mind as reliant on the flow of electrical signals interpreted by the brain. The activity of neuron pathways using electrical impulses was becoming known. Freud was first to speak of the 'unconscious mind' revealed in dreams, which had content that was hidden and disguised from the conscious mind of the individual and remained subliminal.

Freud forwarded a three-part division of the psyche. The *id* was the source of primal and sexual impulses and the main source of psychic energy. In an ordinary individual, it was suppressed and held in check by the *superego* (a socially inculcated awareness of what is moral and appropriate). The *ego*, or active self-awareness and seat of the intellect, existed amid this struggle to fulfil certain basic and sexual desires and satisfy a certain socially inculcated sense of what was right and proper. If the system did not function healthily, suppressed content could dam up psychic energy at the unconscious level and neurosis could develop. Freud wrote critically on religion in *The Future of an Illusion*. Like many others, he saw science as supplanting any need for religion.

His students took his study further and in several directions. Wilhelm Reich saw all energy in all the universe as basically sexual in nature and claimed to have isolated 'Cosmic Orgone Energy'. He represented his 'common functioning principle' symbolically like a capital 'Y', showing how opposites unite.

Alfred Adler saw the primary drive as not necessarily primarily sexual but taking the form of a 'will to power', each individual seeking dominance and acting to relieve feelings of inferiority. This meshed with the 'will to power' theme in philosophy, notably in Nietzsche.

Carl Jung saw all human achievements as the result of 'canalising the libido', that is, diverting the basically sexual energy into other pursuits in the life of the mind and of the individual. He also gave rise to a much broader concept of the unconscious mind by theorising a collective level of the unconscious mind in which potent mythological archetypes had a semi—independent existence, 'the Collective Unconscious'.

Jung also forwarded the theory of 'synchronicity', a non-causal theory of meaningful coincidence. If, for example, he was thinking on the fish as a symbol and came across a school of fish washed up near a lake (which is his own true life example) it was not that his thoughts had caused the fish to wash up but that there was a hidden pattern and interconnectedness in inner and outer events.

Jung recorded conversations with his guardian angel Awaiz.

Toward the end of his life, inspired by Einstein, whom he had met, and the idea that the inter-conversion of energy and matter had a parallel truth in psychology, he theorised that matter had another aspect, a psychic aspect.

What I propose to do is to relate a theory of the 'psycho-spiritual', which takes into account the advances made by psychology in understanding the human mind but also the reality of spiritual phenomena, regarded as the impressions of the unity of all beings and all minds in all space-time—within the ultimate reality of the unity of all in eternity.

In our age, what was once the collective unconscious is transforming into the collective super-consciousness, as it moves further into the conscious awareness of an ever greater numbers of individuals throughout the world. In gaining this awareness, we must look at themes that were earlier suppressed as being too threatening to dwell upon. The idea of super-consciousness gives us at least a psycho-spiritual parallel explanation for the heavenly awareness of self-knowing beings within the greater being of God (angelic awareness).

Many will prefer to think of this as a 'new age' state of awareness humankind has been evolving towards—an age of greater unity and enhanced psychic communication. But it will be far more than that, as it expands awareness towards ultimate reality inclusive of all, in all space-time, so including the phenomena of spirit. Spiritual phenomena have been excluded from psychology and Psychiatry, which deny the existence of spirits as taught by Christ and believed in by a majority of the world's independent cultures and shaman.

I was not born in the time of the Second World War, for which I feel lucky. I was a child of the 1960s. But with the benefit of this comfortable retrospect, I can contemplate the psycho-spiritual factors involved in those times, which to an earlier generation may have been repressed as too frightening to face.

What was it that emerged in the collective psyche of Germany to give rise to the unprecedented levels of inhumanity in the Nazi era? What happened spiritually to allow millions of 'social rejects', including six million Jews (more than half being children) to be slaughtered? What was it as a psycho-spiritual composite that fell into the spiritual vacuum created by scientism (religious adherence to popular science in place of other religion) including Freud, popular atheism based on Nietzsche, and a theology of God as 'utterly other' (to use the German, Rudolph Otto's, words). The problem is not a simple one. For it was a beast of a composite nature, a hybrid of active influences. These are best examined in the light of the Christian tradition, which certainly was the relevant tradition of Germany. At one time, all German kings were automatically Holy Roman emperors. German Catholic efforts to civilise and convert the world to Christianity are well known, and through Martin Luther, Germany gave birth to Protestantism.

The theme of Goethe's *Faust* was a pact with the Devil in return for power. A theme which was to haunt Germany. Lucifer is the angel in rebellion against the Lord's throne. His influence was best represented by Nietzsche who was happy to style himself an Antichrist and gave an egotistic appeal to the will to power. His 'death of God' philosophy became a popular blasphemy in intellectual circles. In a mockery of the true prophet, Zarathustra, who led The Magi to the manger, he sowed the seeds of the Nazi superman myth, predicting a tyrant superman would arise in an age of war.

Fallen Christian angels, who desired vengeance against the Jews for ignoring the Christian message and crucifying Jesus (it is futile to blame anyone for what the Lord knew must be accomplished). These angels were represented in both Catholic and Protestant churches up to WW2. Only Dietrich Bonheoffer the Lutheran Priest who opposed the Nazis as evil and the Jehovah's Witnesses who also published tracts about the Nazi evil rate honourable mention for Christian opposition to the Nazi beast in Germany. While the Church of England had its finest hour as the keepers of the Grail, and American Protestantism proved its purpose.

Satan, the spiritual composite hybrid of human and snake, who gives rise to a strike first without thought influence represented best by Hitler himself (though he also had a wolf spirit). If the nature of the Nuremberg defence—that all were acting on orders—is accepted, this one man wears ultimate responsibility for the death of millions of civilians and hundreds of millions of fatalities in the war he precipitated. The beast, though, was a composite hybrid of enemies of humankind, God, and the Jews sufficient to possess a nation and not only one man. All of these corrupted and guided a dragon spirit power. The dragon is a powerful and powerfully combatant spirit with its own grievance against humanity in general and against God, for causing its extinction. The British imperial dragon and the Japanese imperial dragon were also caught up in the Second World War.

A tragic second wave of 'death of God' philosophy came not from Nietzsche but in the post-war period from Jews, such as Ellie Wessel (Shoah survivor), who could no longer believe in a compassionate and all-powerful God as a result of the Shoah. Even philosophers like Bertrand Russell, who taught metaphysics, including Leibnitz and his theory of compossibles, became post-war atheists. The enemies of the Lord God had almost triumphed firstly by influencing the intellectual and spiritual climate then making such a great evil appear as a result that many could not see humanity as guided by a good and loving God. However, in the balance of powers as we all know, the prevailing Good of the balance, the Lords Way, the Nazis finally lost.

Inhumane empires are such because they are not merely ruled by humans.

A dragon, to me, is not merely a symbol, or an archetype, as in its treatment by Jung (where he thought it could symbolise the mother or the mother earth) but primarily a type of being that once really existed as several related species. Since it was once an existent being, then within the ultimate reality of the unity of all in eternity, in all space-time, it is still a factor in the psycho-spiritual reality. But what we make of impressions of this spiritual reality is not independent of the mind and its concepts. Therefore, we must always speak more correctly of the psycho-spiritual in preference to conceiving of a purely psychic or purely spiritual reality, as we move towards more perfectly conceiving ultimate reality and our relationship with it.

Such psycho-spiritual factors as I have described here have already been largely undone, purified, bound, and some dispensed with, to enable a world in relative peace in the new millennia. This was achieved by human angels who mastered the science of metaphysics or, if you prefer, metaphysical shaman who gained divine awareness of being in God. Do you share in God's responsibility for all events in all time? This is not to say guilt, but there is no way to being in God by avoiding greater responsibility. Being One with God is not all bliss, not considering that the past is with us in Eternity. We now move into a far more hopeful millennia when even psycho-spiritual sensitivities will not believe in the reality of active evil powers in spirit because they will have no power, where human errors are merely the result of 'human error' and not coercive and dangerous spiritual influences.

Chapter 23

DIVINE METAPHYSICS: THE ANGELIC SCIENCE

'Is it not written in your law, "I said Ye are Elohim"' (John 10:34)
(rectified words of Jesus quoting Psalm 82:6).

'THEY KNOW NOT, neither will they understand; they walk on in darkness:
all the foundations of the earth are out of course. I have said, Ye are Elohim
and all of you are children of the most High (Psalm 82:5-6).

In Christian thought, but also in Jewish, Zoroastrian, and Islamic thought,
angels are divine beings intermediate between humankind and God.
Although I intend to lead on to a metaphysical treatment of angels, I shall
begin with 'angelology', a known area of religious study in comparative
religion.

Angels were known in Old Testament Judaic times only as messengers of
God. The Hebrew word is *maloak* (messenger). In the most significant roles,
an angel in human form visited Abraham and Sarah to give them news of
her miracle birth (since she was old and barren) of Isaac. Angels visited Lot
in human form to warn him of the impending destruction of Sodom.

Jacob, resting at Bethel ('house of God', the name he gave the place), dreamed
of a ladder that reached to heaven, with angels ascending and descending
on it and the Lord God above it (Genesis 28). Later, he wrestled with a
man/angel/messenger at *Peniel* (Face of God; this angel's name) (Genesis
32). Jacob prevailed and was given the name *Yisrael* (God prevails), which
sounds like an angel's name of the familiar form incorporating the Hebrew

'El' for God. Jacob had his own covenant (established on Abraham's and Isaac's), and possibly the angel Peniel could not overcome him as being dependant on his angel enabling covenant through which his 12 sons became the lineage of the twelve tribes of Judaic angels predominately male, or *Bene Elohim* (Sons of God, Sons of Light). Thus Joseph the angel *Yisrael* actually enabled the Lord God of angel hosts in Unity with and as *Elohim*. This explains the following scripture-

'Yea, he had power over the angel, and prevailed: he wept, and made supplication unto him: he found him in Bethel, and there he spake with us; Even the LORD God of hosts; the LORD is his memorial' (Hosea 12:4).

The angel (*Elohim*) of Yehovah appeared to Moses in the burning bush in spirit form to give him this name of the Lord God and subsequently led the children of Israel through the wilderness in their Exodus from Egypt.

Daniel was instructed by angels, in spirit form, including *Michael*, who had to fight his way through the 'prince of the east' (probably *Marduk* since he was in Babylon, though he may also be equated with or identified as *Lucifer*, a dragon-man confluence hybrid). *Gabriel* also instructed him.

Angels, including *Gabriel*, announced and attended the birth of Jesus and assisted at his Resurrection and ascension. The 'Star of Bethlehem' itself may have been an angelic host, since it could lead to and hover above a manger for the Magi to follow.

There are only two definitive named angels in the protestant canonical Old Testament—*Michael* ('who is like God', a warring prince) and *Gabriel* ('God is great', a prophetic messenger), both in the book of Daniel. *Raphael* ('God's healing', the healer) is named in the book of Tobit, and *Uriel* ('God is my light', the fire of God, or hell's guardian) in II Esdras. (Tobit and Esdras are found in the Catholic Bible.) Uriel might be equated with *Abbadon* (Greek) or *Apollyon* from Revelations 9:11 who may have a similar role in hell.

Lucifer, the fallen angel, who attempted to raise himself above the stars of God, is only mentioned in Isaiah (14:12), though he is referred to as a man and linked to the empire of Babylon.

Seraphim, the fiery ones, the mysterious six-winged angels who attend on the Lord, are only mentioned in Isaiah 6, where Isaiah is given his prophetic commission in a vision.

Cherubim with flaming sword are involved in the exile of Adam and Eve from Eden in Genesis, depicted on the Ark of the Covenant in the Exodus and in Solomon's Temple. Although their depiction is uncertain, they are sometimes envisaged like winged sphinx or human animal hybrids, and *Cherubim* are identified in Ezekiel's vision as the winged 'living creatures' with the faces of a man, a lion, an ox, and an eagle (Ezekiel 1 and 10). The artistic tradition of envisaging them as childlike angels emerged later, as in Christ's reshaping of heaven, I believe this spiritual reality changed.

Kabbalistic mystics and mages used *Michael, Gabriel, Raphael,* and *Uriel* as the four archangels of the four quarters identified with the four elementals, and this entered the iconography of Catholicism.

There was also a variety of Jewish mysticism (Merkabah) that developed the concept of seven archangels (seven regarded as the complete number by the Jews), angels who protected various levels of heavenly ascent. Seven archangels are mentioned in the book of Tobit.

In Zoroastrianism, there are also seven chief angelic beings or *amesha spentas* each having the assigned character of the chief divine virtues. My interpretation of an idea found in Zoroastrianism is that human mortals, could by passing through a test of fire (molten metal in the inner earth) and conjoined with the most holy spirit in the heavens, become angel-like beings.

In Islam, there are four throne bearers of Allah, along with Jibal (Gabriel?), angel of revelation; Mikal (Michael?), here an angel of knowledge of nature; Izra'il (Uriel or Yisrael?), the angel of death; and Israfil (Raphael?), who sounds the trumpet of judgement and places the immortal soul in the body.

These are only the chief named angels, and all these religions recognise other or lower order angels. In Christianity, Judaism, and Islam, one theory has been of 'the great chain of being'—that angels are a separately created and superior form of being to humanity. However there is little in the way of scriptural support for this theory and some indications to the contrary given in the teachings of Jesus.

When Jesus regards children, speaking fondly of 'the angels of these little ones' and says they always are close to the Lord God in heaven, it could be interpreted in a number of different ways.

One established Catholic Church belief is that everyone has his or her own guardian angel. However, we may regard these guardian angels as simply the ascendant spirit or higher spiritual nature of the children. Guardian angels may be our own angel nature, existing eternally as one with God before we become aware of our eternal identity with them. Though other angels may assist us.

There is general agreement that only the purest spirits come close to the Lord in heaven. Jesus taught his followers to become again like children to enter the kingdom of heaven.

In Mark 12:25, as well as in Matthew 22:30 and Luke 20:34, Jesus makes the promise that in the Resurrection or the aeon to come (in Luke) those found worthy shall live as the angels or equal to them. We are all necessary equals within the necessary unity of all in all eternity, Each with the Logos mind of God within; we are all Elohim, children of God, angels of light, each holding within the necessary balance, which resembles, approaches, and finally becomes one with the innermost balance of nature, the Way of nature, and the prevailing Way in all events.

In my reading of scripture, it is not necessary to die in order to become an angel; the heavenly kingdom is primarily a kingdom of the living, and the forceful take it by force. Here, though, I shed my scholar's robe and speak also as a metaphysician, with the benefit of spiritual and angelic experience. It has been enabled by my new covenant that humans become angels while they live and breathe (to follow).

Another metaphysician has touched on similar ground, Emanuel Swedenborg wrote of men elevated by divine love to an angelic state and of angelic awareness set in the eternal and not the ordinary passage of time.

God has so arranged it that there is no stronger force, principle, or power than love, and the power of Love cannot be abused since it is available only to those who love. The supreme force of love is at its strongest in purity of spirit. However, it is not an aseptic 'charity' but a love desiring union.

The Lord had plans for a reconstitution of heaven in the new Millennia, in which, strangely, the newest of angels to join the throng are regarded as superior to those who came before. He stated that never among men was there born anyone greater than John the Baptist, himself referred to in scripture as an angel preparing the Way, yet he would be least in the kingdom of heaven.

The angels of the new aeon are superior, since they are born in a more perfect age, where they could identify with the greater unity of God, uncorrupted by the defeated evils of the last age and having greater awareness. However, a category of transitional angels (in which I include myself) had to struggle for this victory and also to reconcile spirits to being in God. Here I must admit to having been formerly a shaman, able to spirit travel, before gaining, in stages, divine awareness of being in God through the Lord.

An angel of this age, being a human in this age, not only may live and rule with Christ a thousand years in the millennia ahead but, in a sense, does so eternally. Only as one with Christ, Yeshua, may we say, 'I am the Alpha and Omega, the first and the last'.

The awareness of angels passes beyond time and involves a seeming paradox of being an active influence in times past. Though this might easily be equated with our pre-existent being, there is a sense in which something has come to fruition in this age that has always been the world's best making and shaping influence in the retrospective cycle of time. A meta-logic of time paradox has been developed in Equipoise principle patterns and will be further developed in this millennia to account definitively for how the perfected Lord God and his angelic Elohim from this aeon have always made and shaped all things from the beginning. As Logos understands Logos, God becomes fully self-aware through us.

We offer up our gifts to the giver of all good gifts, the Lord God in the person of Jesus born of Bethlehem who, by his covenant-making sacrifice, reconciled all beings to being in God.

Beautiful are the feet of angels who walk upon this earth in our age. They are the first fruits of the Lords Millennial Rule and the kingdom of heaven.

There is a heavenly elect, who are also pure and childlike. But the next ascendant angels to enter heaven and unite with the Lord, though young, may well find themselves placed in charge of nations, superior in authority to the prophets and set above the churches. Heaven has something of the nature of a 'juniocracy'; it is ruled by children or those indistinguishable from children, who have resumed the nature of their child selves and souls. Ageism (discrimination on the basis of age) will be the next form of prejudice and oppression to be eliminated throughout the earth, following Racism and Sexism.

Our original self, mind, and soul is in the nature of Logos, the nature of the Lord. Implicit in it is the ability to distinguish and make choices. Freedom is an implicit principle deriving from the first principle. We unite with the Lord, and we find in this union not a demolition of selfhood but an affirmation of that which we have always considered to be our most essential selfhood.

The angel raptures of ineffable bliss and freedom in being *Elohim*, one with God, have to be experienced to be believed. We need not stick to quoting scripture. We are not commanded, but only gently led. The Lord, having been unified with us, entrusts us with his power and authority, so that angels are more than messengers but may speak for God.

He is the gentlest, loving Lord and teaches us to hold power, likewise, gently. As an angelic Elohim, one with God, you can go anywhere in time or space; communicate, identify and unify with any person, people, creatures, or forces of nature to influence them; and share awareness. This is ultimate freedom.

In the inner heavens, angels sometimes play like loving children immersed in a purity of love in spirit that unifies them. In short, it's way cool.

There are only some constraints on angelic freedom, which hang on necessary consequence. All beings have freedom implicit through the Logos form of mind and soul and are able to make errors. Angels can forgive sins, but if they should do so carte blanche, they will end up wearing a spiritual burden, which may cost them their ascendancy. Jesus gave his apostles the right to forgive or retain sins (John 20:23). But in an ordinary sense, we should not want to retain them. It is best to only forgive specific errors freely acknowledged as errors, in the business of angelic judgement and healing. This is the angelic angle on the doctrine of grace—that only sins recognised and admitted can be forgiven, not unacknowledged errors in unawareness. Justice necessitates the perfect balance between tolerance and intolerance.

In our age, the Lord is more truly omnipotent than ever before, having less active adversaries and control of all powers. The general shape of the New Age Covenant is in fulfilment of the prophecy of Ephesians 1:10 that all beings in heaven and earth are becoming subsumed by the Lord himself in the 'fullness of his times'. All are fish in the greater ocean of God's being, all but the fishermen and fisherwomen, and this is the way of the angels.

I will tell you a true story of my angelic experience around 2004. A certain angel tried to stand over me and demanded I ask permission for things, and I threw this angel down as a demon of hierarchy. When suppressed under me, he kept asking me permission for things. It took him some time to reform his idea of hierarchy.

On earth, the reform of hierarchical structures, which oppress humanity and curtail freedom and equality, is the next step in overcoming evident forms of evil inherited from the 'principalities and powers' of the previous age.

I was also both spiritual witness and angelic participant to the binding of the winged dragon and the defeat and binding of Satan (a snake-man confluence hybrid being), which began this millennial rule of Christ's kingdom over the earth after ten complete years of spiritual warfare. Lucifer the deceiver was, in prospect, bound a thousand years since he was an angel of sorts and not easily dispensed with, but he returned on the retrospective. A more permanent solution was found in retrospectively binding and reconciling the water dragon, Leviathan (Nessie the Pleosaur), which Marduk slew to disempower the Babylon lineage which has caused a worldwide influence of oppression and inequality. I predict the Lords Millennial Rule should become evident from 2112 onward.

An angel's existence is both necessary and contingent—upon the Lord in the person of Jesus firstly, but also on each other in a contingent network. We are creature-creators, *Elohim* eternally one with the Lord. While you contend with the mystery of human angels living among us, consider this: As an angel involved in the Lord's ascension by his host (including some angels not yet born), I know the purpose of the ascension was not to lift the Lord through space, but through space-time, into our millennia. He works as he will, and no man or angel can prophecy his return.

After being through the Lord's baptism of fire, which is both the earth's molten core (for some) and spiritual flames, which heal and purify, we can realise our angelic birth right and highest potential. Though only with the unifying power of love can we unite with the Lord, through loving him who has enabled all things foremost. Angel *Elohim* have immortal spiritual bodies of light, which radiate light to look somewhat like wings, which they are given in artistic convention. But these are not wings of feathers. Don't let the mythology of angels blind you to their spiritual reality.

You are all *Elohim*, actual or potential angels one with God, and children of the most high God. The Ever-becoming One is reaching a new stage of perfection eternally attained, and so is the human race, having evolved towards their angelic potential. Aristotle described metaphysics as, 'Being such a science God alone could have, or God before all others', and so it is, finally; *The science of Elohim—the angelic science of divine metaphysics.*

All things have their first and final cause in God, who draws upon the sum of human knowledge for both awareness and self-awareness. God, the eternal being, the Alpha and Omega, through mastery of time paradox, involved our perfected awareness of natural science and metaphysics to create all things in the beginning.

'In the beginning *Elohim* created the heavens and the earth' (Genesis 1:1). (The word 'God' restored to the Hebrew original)

It is my purpose to deliver this Covenant, such as it is, to this Age. You may take this covenant as a simple affirmation or, more ceremonially and effectively, enter into it by the shedding of a couple of drops of your own blood for the healing of nations and the reconciliation of spirits, within the Equipoise symbol (don't hurt yourself a small cut on the back of the arm will suffice). This is an angel enabling Covenant built on the linage of Covenants including Christ the Lord's, its duration is 2000 years, and beyond. It can be built on but not subtracted from as Covenant Law has a history of precedent.

THE NEW AGE COVENANT

We who are many in God unite;

We share a common purpose—

To serve and maintain the innermost balance of nature,

The innermost of the innermost,

Where the implied two meet and conjoin,

In the unity of the All in One and One in All.

In and through Christ the Lord,

Logos masters Chaos.

The Lord rules in perfect balance.

God is Love; Love unifies.

Love unites the opposites.

Love maintains the balance.

Love protects the innocent.

We maintain the balanced Good,

The balanced Truth made perfect.

Departing not into extremes,

Peace prevails over conflict.

Let us be as the one above,

The Lord who reigns and rules,

United in the Lord as God,

Elohim, angels,

Prevailing in the Way Eternal.

Chapter 24

EQUIPOISE DIVINE GEOMETRY

Figure 24.1 Equipoise and its relation to the Tai Chi or Yin—Yang diagram.

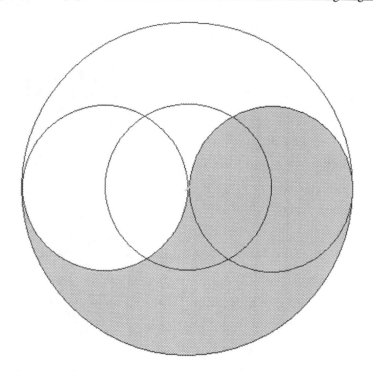

See how the Equipoise Symbol, located centrally within the above diagram, becomes a symbol of limited infinity (paradox intended). After you colour either the left or right circle darker, and a tail after it (as shown above), on either the retrospective or progressive cycles, you then have something like a yin-yang or tai chi diagram (though on its side). The Equipoise key Principle Pattern is, then, the symbol of the innermost balance of nature and of the eternal and prevailing Way. The three interlocked circles are a symbol of the Pythagorean Triad which divide the central Monad into its Logos pattern. The Equipoise key Symbol is not a traditional Pythagorean Symbol, but relates to them.

Figure 24.2 The Vescia Pisces or Pisces Symbol and it relation to the Equipoise Key Symbol

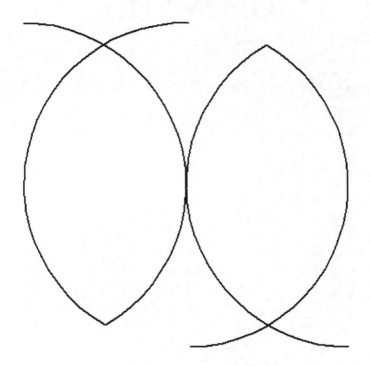

The symbols above show the *vesica piscis*, the 'vessel of the fish' or Pisces Symbol from its origin in the Equipoise key. It shows how the fish of Pisces, an early Christian symbol, swim deep within the ocean of the Key to Aquarius, the Equipoise key. All are fish within the ocean of God's greater being, all but the fisherman. This is the Way of *Elohim*, the Way of the angels, the prevailing Way. Yet it is not easy to teach fish to be fishermen or fisherwomen.

Figure 24.3 The Mandorla as found within the Equipoise Key Symbol

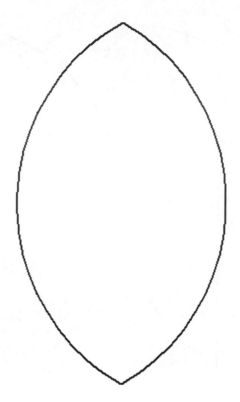

The mandorla (almond in Latin) pattern, when derived true from compass in an equipoise key of any size, has constant proportions of width to height of one to the square root of three, as does a rectangle within the central dipole pattern defined by its corners of intersection (the 'inner door').

Figure 24.4 The Inner Door within the Equipoise Key

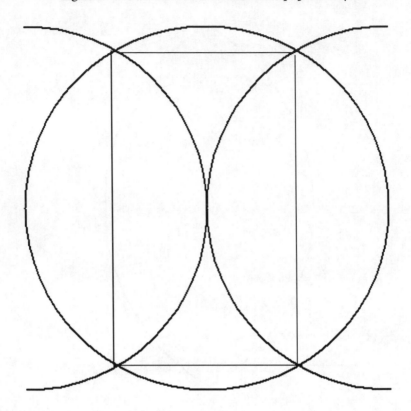

The *Inner Door* depicted above within the Equipoise Key diagram also has constant proportions of width to height of one to the square root of three like the *mandorla*. "Yea though I stand at the door and Knock"

Figure 24.5 Equipoise Key diagram divided into six sectors of 60 degrees

The squared circle proportions below provide, along with the two points, which are your compass points, in drawing an equally divided circle in six sectors of 60 degrees in the Magian measure.

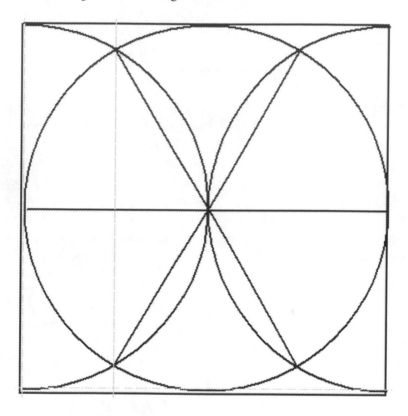

You see why gravity should allow for up to 30 degrees of departure from the perpendicular. But 23.3 degrees of inclination from perpendicular is too much for this earth, and we need the help of all angels to minimise it to about 17.5 degrees in the next millennium. This will restore the earth to Equipoise conditions, countering global warming, greenhouse gas emissions, and minimising temperature extremes. It is the *Equipoise project* to minimise extremes in all things and restore balance. This is an ambitious on-going millennial project, which needs further work and development. We inherit the Care of the earth and maintenance of nature's balance, in and from, God.

'They know not, neither will they understand; they walk on in darkness: all *the foundations of the earth are out of course*. I have said, Ye are *Elohim* and all of you are children of the most High' (Psalm 82:5-6).

{Emphasis added the Elohim Charter from the Psalms speaks of the earth out of course }

Figure 24.5 The Blue Dragon (Retrospective Cycle) and the Red Dragon's (Progressive cycle) Binding

The diagram below shows how the two dragons are bound. The dragon on the retrospective cycle is a *blue dragon* and female. The dragon on the progressive cycle is a *red dragon* and male. They are both bound in the Equipoise key. Those who take the covenant assist in the binding of the dragons which are actually hosts of females and hosts of males in spirit united by Love, and bound to the innermost balance of nature (they had previously been bound to the Tao by Taoists). They enable a sort of empowerment, and because bound on the Chronos pattern are linked to space-time travel.

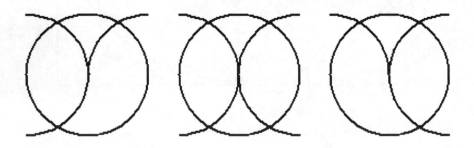

Spirit of the risen Christ Yeshua. Prince of Peace. Lord of Love. Lord of the perfect balance enabled by Love. Bless Us, Heal us, Cleanse us. Keep us in peace. Unite us to the truth of being in God as angel Elohim with Love that unifies, and guide us in your perfect Way that we may not depart from it neither to the left, nor to the right. Let it Be.

Poetry Appendix

To my Angel beloved

If this be not love, there is no love,
Neither on earth nor the realm above.
If this love be not true, there is no truth,
And the sacred surrenders to the uncouth;
The truth is, I love you. It is always the same—
The transient passes; the truth shall remain.

* * *

To the New Phoenix

From the ashes of your former self . . . Arise!
From the grave which was your nesting place,
From the fire of your death . . . Arise!
Born of Earth, the Sky is your domain.
Beautiful creature, stretch your Golden wings and fly;
Gaze at sun and moon with eyes unblinking . . . All space is yours. Arise!

* * *

Old Dragon

Ancient one, we met opposed,

I knew you as the adversary of man,

But with this verse I have composed,

I'll talk straight of how our battle ran.

I saw your ancient spirit descend,

Bathed in light, an angel of a different kind;

Some thought the world approached its end,

As you kindled fire in their minds.

By Heaven's will, I held the rod of Aaron,

And it sprouted streams of fiery light,

And as the angels forced you down,

We conjoined the age-old fight.

But how can eternal spirits die?

Or prison be made for beings of the Sky?

And as the dragon slayers found why,

A dragon slain, is then that dragon I.

We forced you down within the earth;

I set a binding seal upon the ground.

The earth corrupt was nature's dearth,

As more awful form you found.

The sickening reach of pit-bound beast,

A beast who bayed for human blood,

Reached upward, not to me the least,

And threatened mankind with its evil flood.

You opened prospect portals then and now,

But then were filled with soulless pain,

The death of innocents was how,

All innocence would find its drain.

There was no choice, no way but one—

We found concordance on a plan,

The seal amended, no one won;

What binds the dragon binds the man.

Fools rush in, it's truly said, where angels fear to tread;

I stood within a balanced sign,

Containment opened, awestruck, filled with dread.

With certain words, We made your binding mine.

'Bound within the boundless', so it chants,

And straight talk became the truth 'tween you and I;

The truth is that though struggle and concordance,

Peace prevailed, and then you took me to the Sky.

Did humans kill your kind old ones and slay your young?

'Tis evil too, much like the millions slain by you.

We know the truth of God is all in one,

The truth of union greater than the two.

Unconquerable spirit, you are wise.

Through ages, you have known our best and seen our worst;

You've shown me truth through dragon's eyes,

Though cyclic time I met you last, and yet I knew you first.

For us, old one, the Age has just begun,

And for an age united, where the two are one,

We'll guide all souls and do what must be done,

Beneath Christ's throne, and who'd have thought it run

'Twas the final battle 'tween good and evil,
 and yet ... the fool won.

I am a fool. I know one thing; that's All ... agnoi.

Bibliography

Chapter 1. The Way of Nature

Ancient(unknown) (1951 trans) The I Ching, or Book of Changes
(Richard Wilhelm Trans -Cary Barnes Eng Trans) London :
Routledge & K.Paul

Chan, Wing-tsit. (1963). *A Sourcebook in Chinese Philosophy*. Princetown,
N.J: Princetown University Press. (Every Quotation in the Chapter is
from this excellent sourcebook)

Chuang-tzu (1996) *The Book of Chuang-tzu*. (Martin Palmer Trans,
with Elizabeth Breuilly, Chang Wai Ming and Jay Ramsay) London :
Penguin

Lao-tzu (2000) *The Teachings of Lao-tzu: The Tao te Ching*. (Paul Carus
Trans) London: Rider

Lao-tzu. (1992). *Tao te ching:The book of the Way and its virtue*. (J.
Duyvendak, Trans.) Boston: C E Tuttle Co.

Lao-tzu. (1997). *Tao te Ching*. (J. Legge, Trans.) Mineola, N.Y: Dover
Publications.

Lao-tzu. (1999). *Tao te Ching*. (T. Freke, Trans.) London: Piatkus.

Chapter 2. The Way of the Shaman

Castaneda, Carlos (1993) *The art of dreaming*. New York : Harper Collins

Castaneda, Carlos (1990) The Teachings of Don Juan: a Yaqui way of
knowledge. New York, Sydney: Washington Square Press

Eliade, M. (1973). *Australian Religions an Introduction*. Cornell: Ithica

Eliade, M. (1964). *Shamanism: archaic techniques of ecstasy*. London :
Routledge & K.Paul

Elkin, A.P (1945) *Aboriginal men of high degree*, Sydney:
Australasian Publishing

Halifax, J. (1980). *Shamanic voices: a survey of visionary narratives.* Harmondsworth : Penguin

Mathews, Caitlin (1994) *The Encyclopaedia of Celtic Wisdom: the Celtic shaman's sourcebook* (Caitlin & John Mathews) Shaftsbury, Dorset, Brisbane Qld : Element

Nicholson, Shirley (1989) *Shamanism,* New York : Theosophical Society Publishing (Black Elk Quote)

CHAPTER 3. THE WAY OF THE BRAHMIN

Buddha (2005) *The Dhammapada : teachings of the Buddha* (Gil Fronsdal Trans) Boston : Shambhala

Buddha (1950) *The Dhammapada : with introductory essays* (S. Radhakrishnan Trans) London : Oxford University Press

Chan, Wing-tsit. (1963). *A Sourcebook in Chinese Philosophy.* Princetown, N.J: Princetown University Press. (Shen-Hui—Zen Buddhist quote)

Mukopadhyay, K.L. (1968) *Introduction to Shankara.* Calcutta, IP

Prebish, C.S & Keown, D. (2110) *Introducing Buddhism.* London : Routledge

Smart, N. (1977) *The Long search.* Boston : Little, Brown

Sundara-Ramiah, G.(1974) *Brahman-a comparative study of the philosophies of Sankara and Ramanuja* Waltair, Andhra University Press

Thomas, E.J. (1992) *The Song of the Lord—Bhagavadgita.* Boston: C.E. Tuttle

Zaehner, R.C (1966). *Hindu Scriptures.* London: Dent—Everyone's Library

CHAPTER 4. THE WAY OF THE MAGI

Boyce, Mary (1979) *Zoroastrians their religious beliefs and practices.* London, Boston: Routledge & Kegan Paul

Revealed (1611) *The King James Bible,* Authorised Version (trans team following on W. Tyndale trans)

Rose, Jenny (2011) *Zoroastrianism : a guide for the perplexed.* London : Continuum

Herodotus, added author De Selencourt A. (1966) *The Histories.* Harmondsworth : Penguin Books

Xenaphon, added author Antrich, J. Usher, S. (1978) *The Persian Expedition*, Bristol :Bristol Classic Press

Zoroaster (1948 trans) *The Hymns of Zarathustra-being a translation of the Gathas* (Duchesne-Guillemin, Jacques. Trans to French) (Henning, M. Trans to English) 1st Edition, London J.Murray (1952) London : Wisdom of the East Series (All Yasna Quotes)

Chapter 5. The Way of the Philosophers

Aristotle (1998 trans) *The Metaphysics* (Lawson-Tancred, Hugh Trans & added author).London: Penguin

Guthrie, K.S.(1987) *The Pythagorean Sourcebook and Library : a collection of ancient writings which Relate to Pythagoras and Pythagorean Philosophy*. Grand Rapids : Phanes Press

Kenny, A (1994) *The Oxford History of Western Philosophy*. New York: Oxford University Press

Russel, B (1946) *History of Western Philosophy and its connection with political and social circumstances from earliest times to the present day*. London: G.Allen & Unwin (source of translated quotes of ancient Greek philosophers)

Magee, Brian (1998) *The Story of Philosophy*. London : Dorling Kindersley

Smart, N (1999) *World Philosophies*. London, New York: Routledge

Chapter 6. The Way out of Egypt

Budge, E.A.W (1971) *Egyptian magic* (reprint of 1901 edition, Sir Ernest Alfred Wallis Budge) New York: Dover Publications (Accounts of Egyptian Magic)

Copenhaver, B.P.(1992) *Hermetica : the Greek Corpus Hermeticum and Latin Asclepius* (Brian Copenhaver Trans) New York : Cambridge University Press

Faulkner, R.O. (1973-1978) *The Ancient Egyptian Coffin Texts*. (R.O Faulkner Trans), Warminster: Aris & Phillips (Source of all Coffin text Quotations)

Freke, Timothy (1997) *The Hermetica the lost wisdom of the Pharoahs* (T.Freke & P. Gandy) London : Piatcus

Iversen, Erik (1984) *Egyptian and Hermetic Doctrine*. Copenhagen : Museum Tusculanum

Pritchard, James (2110) *The ancient Near East : an anthology of texts and pictures*. Princeton N.J: Princeton University Press (Memphite Theology)

Valantasis, R. (1997) *The Gospel of Thomas* (Valantasis, R. Trans) London, New York : Routledge

Chapter 7. Druidism—Preparing the Way

Barber, Richard (1999) *Myths and legends of the British Isles*. Woodbridge, Suffolk : Boydell Press

Mathews, Caitlin (1994) *The Encyclopaedia of Celtic Wisdom: the Celtic shaman's sourcebook* (Caitlin & John Mathews) Shaftsbury, Dorset, Brisbane Qld: Element

Mathews, John (1996) *The Druid Sourcebook : from earliest times to the present day*. London : Blandford Press: Distributed U.S.A New York, Stirling Press (all quotes from this source)

Piggot, S. (1985) *The Druids*. New York: Thames and Hudson

Chapter 8. The Way of The Prophets

Revealed (1611) *The King James Bible*, Authorised Version (trans team following on W. Tyndale trans)

Revealed (2000) *Nelsons Bible Reference Library* (C.D Rom), Thomas Nelson Publishers, Tennessee

Thanks and acknowledgement to Thomas Nelson for this invaluable resource which incorporates a Strong's Concordance and Hebrew and Greek dictionaries

Chapter 9. The Way of The Essenes

Burrows, M (1956). *The Dead Sea Scrolls*. (Burrows, Millar Trans), London :Secker and Warburg

Josephus, Flavius (1988 ed) The Works of Josephus : complete and unabridged ((William Whitson Trans) Peabody Mass : Hendrickson

Vermes, G (1962) *The Dead Sea Scrolls in English* : Harmondsworth : Penguin Books (Dead sea scrolls quotes including Community rules from this source)

Chapter 10. The Way of the Lord & Chapter 11. The Way of the Apostles

Revealed (1611) *The Holy Bible*, King James Authorised Version (team following on W. Tyndale Trans)

Revealed (1982) *The Holy Bible, New King James Version*, Tennessee : Thomas Nelson Publisher (Scripture taken from the New King James Version Copyright 1982 by Thomas Nelson Inc. Used by permission. All rights reserved)

Various (2000) *Nelsons Bible Reference Library* (C.D Rom), Thomas Nelson Publishers, Tennessee

Thanks and acknowledgement to Thomas Nelson for this invaluable resource which incorporates a Strong's Concordance and Hebrew and Greek dictionaries

Chapter 12.The Way of the Sufis

Bullock, A. & Trombley, S. (2000 ?) *The Fontana Dictionary of Modern thought*. London : Fontana 3rd Edition, (entry under 'New World Order')

Jalal Al-din Rumi, M (1940) *The Mathnawi of Jalalu'ddin Rumi* (Nicholson R.A trans) London : E.J. Brill

Nicholson, R.A.(1914) *The Mystics of Islam*. London : G.Bell ('I died as mineral' quote)

Mohammed (2003 ed) *The Koran* (N.J.Dawood Trans) London : Penguin

Shah, I. (1964) *The Sufis*, Garden City N.Y, Doubleday

Smart, N (1999) *World Philosophies*. London, New York: Routledge

Chapter 13. The Way through later Philosophy

Bradley, F.H. (1925) *Appearance and Reality : a metaphysical essay*. London: Allen & Unwin

Descartes, R (1986) *First Meditation*, New York: Cambridge University Press

Kant, I. (1934) (reissued 1991)*Critique of pure reason*,(J.M.D. Meiklejohn Trans). London : Dent

Kant, I (1969) *Foundations of the Metaphysics of morals*,(L.W.Beck Trans) Indianapolis: Bobbs-Merrill

Plantinga, A (1965) *The Ontological argument : from St Anselm to contemporary Philosophers*. New York Doubleday

Russel, B (1946) *History of Western Philosophy and its connection with political and social circumstances from earliest times to the present day.* London: G.Allen & Unwin

Smart, N (1999) *World Philosophies*. London, New York: Routledge

Swedenborg, E. (1970 ed) *The Essential Swedenborg: basic teachings of Emanuel Swedenborg, scientist philosopher, and theologian*. New York : Swedenborg Foundation

CHAPTER 14. THE WAY THROUGH SCIENCE

Christianson, Gale (1984) *In the presence of the Creator : Isaac Newton and his times*. New York : Free Press ; London : Collier Macmillan (Keynes Quotation source)

Bernstein, Dan (2005) *Secrets of Angels and Demons*. (Dan Bernstein & Arne de Keijzer) London: Orion Contains a good interview with Owen Gingerich, 'On the Copernican Trail'

Hawking, S.W (1988) *A Brief History of Time : from the Big Bang to Black Holes*, Toronto, New York: Bantam Books

Koestler, Arthur (1968) *The sleepwalkers : a history of man's changing vision of the universe* Hamondsworth: Penguin ; Pelican books

Newton, I. (1726) (This Ed 1972) *Philosophiae naturalis principia mathematica (Koyre, A Ed)* Cambridge Mass: Harvard University Press

Newton, I (1999) *The Principia : mathematical principles of natural philosophy* (Cohen, I Ed Trans) Berkley: University of California Press

Maury, J.P (1992) *Newton: understanding the cosmos*, London: Thames and Hudson

White, Michael (1997) *Isaac Newton : the last Sorcerer*. London : Fourth Estate (source for Newton's 'Philosophers stone' quote and Newton's Prophecy timescale)

CHAPTER 15. THE WAY THROUGH LATER SCIENCE

Cantor, G. N (1996) *Michael Faraday*. Atlantic Highlands N.J : Humanities Press

Hamilton, J (2003) *Faraday: the life*, London :Harper Collins

Hawking, S.W (1988) *A Brief History of Time : from the Big Bang to Black Holes*, Toronto, New York: Bantam Books

Horgan, John (1977) *The End of Science: facing the limits of knowledge in the twilight of the scientific Age.* London: Little, Brown

Chapter 16. The Way into the New Age

Josephus, Flavius (1988 ed) The Works of Josephus: complete and unabridged ((William Whitson Trans) Peabody Mass: Hendrickson

Revealed (1611) *The Holy Bible*, King James Authorised Version (team following on W. Tyndale Trans)

Revealed (1982) *The Holy Bible, New King James Version*, Tennessee : Thomas Nelson Publisher (Scripture taken from the New King James Version Copyright 1982 by Thomas Nelson Inc. Used by permission. All rights reserved)

Chapter 17. The Way in Divine Metaphysics

Aristotle (1998 trans) *The Metaphysics* (Lawson-Tancred, Hugh Trans & added author). London: Penguin

Chapter 18. The Way in Equipoise

Feyman, Richard.P. (1985) *Q.E.D :the strange theory of light and matter*, Princeton NJ :Princeton University Press

Zukav, Gary (1979) *The Dancing Wu Li Masters: an overview of the new physics*, New York : Morrow

Chapter 19. Equipoise Symbols and the Unified Event

Capra, Fritof (1976) *The Tao of Physics: an exploration of the parallels between modern physics and eastern mysticism*, London: Fontana/ Collins

Feyman, Richard .P. (1985) *Q.E.D :the strange theory of light and matter*, Princeton NJ :Princeton University Press

Hawking, Steven .W (1988) *A Brief History of Time : from the Big Bang to Black Holes*, Toronto, New York: Bantam Books

Zukav, Gary (1979) *The Dancing Wu Li Masters: an overview of the new physics*, New York : Morrow

CHAPTER 20. EQUIPOISE IN THE ETERNAL DREAMING
(own ethnography)

CHAPTER 21. IN SPIRIT AND IN TRUTH

Revealed (1611) *The Holy Bible*, King James Authorised Version (team following on W. Tyndale Trans)

CHAPTER 22. THE PSYCHOSPIRITUAL

Freud, Sigmund (1949) *The ego and the id* (J.Riviere Trans) London : Hogarth Press
Freud, Sigmund (1949) *The Future of an Illusion* (W.D.Robson-Scott Trans) London : Hogarth Press
Jung, C.G. (1978) *Man and his Symbols*. London : Picador
Roazen, P. (1976) *Freud and his followers*. London : Allen Lane
Storr, A. (1973) *Jung*, London. Fontana

CHAPTER 23. DIVINE METAPHYSICS, THE ANGELIC SCIENCE

Aristotle (1998 trans) *The Metaphysics* (Lawson-Tancred, Hugh Trans & added author). London: Penguin
Revealed (1611) *The Holy Bible*, King James Authorised Version (team following on W. Tyndale Trans)
Swedenborg, E (1985) Angelic wisdom concerning divine love and wisdom (G.F. Dole Trans) U.S.A : Swedenborg Foundation
Various (2000) *Nelsons Bible Reference Library* (C.D Rom), Thomas Nelson Publishers, Tennessee
Thanks and acknowledgement to Thomas Nelson for this invaluable resource which incorporates a Strong's Concordance and Hebrew and Greek dictionaries

CHAPTER 24. EQUIPOISE AND DIVINE GEOMETRY

Lundy, M (2001) Sacred Geometry : New York : Walker and Co

Index

P

Pacelli, Cardinal, 100
panentheist, 40
pantheism, 79, 82
Parmenides, 29–30, 106
Paul (apostle), 4, 32, 39–40, 64, 67–70, 83, 100
Pentecost, 67–68
Peripatetics, 84, 87, 92
Peter (apostle), 66–69, 101
phenomena, 9, 11, 15, 28, 80, 92, 97, 113, 143, 152
philosophy, 14–16, 19, 29–30, 80–83, 87
photon, 127
Plato, 29–31, 74, 84
pneuma, 142
positivism, 92
positron, 126
prayer, xi, 42, 62, 148
principle, 5–6, 107–8, 110, 120–23, 125–27, 130–34, 166
Principle Patterns, 120
progressive, 115, 125, 127, 132, 170
prophecy, 22–24, 45, 49, 52–53, 55, 58, 66, 69, 98
prophet, 63, 72
prophets, 64, 72
prospects, 79–80
proton, 129
psychology, 84, 115, 150–52
psycho-spiritual, 115, 150–52, 154
pure, 2, 9, 38, 80
purify, 11, 147, 162
purity, 11
Pythagoras, 26–29, 31, 44, 84–86

Q

quest, 16, 46

R

Rachel (angel), 96
Ramanuja, 14–16
Raphael (angel), 156–57
religion, x, xiii, 7, 10, 20–21, 23, 27, 30, 34–35, 46–47, 71–73, 75–76, 98–99, 105–6, 151–52
retrospective, 115, 126–27, 133, 170
Rumi, 75
Russell, Bertrand, 82, 154
Rutherford, Ernest, 93
Ruwach, 51

S

Sankara, 14–15, 18
Sartre, Jean-Paul, 83
Satan, 26, 145, 153, 161
Saxons, 45–46
Schopenhauer, Arthur, 81
Schrödinger, Erwin, 95
Seraph, 144
seraphim, 50, 157
serpent, 139
shaman, 7–8, 11, 63, 146
shamanism, 7, 12
Sikh, 75
sin, 30, 62, 102, 146
snake, 138, 141, 153, 161
Socrates, 30–31, 70
Solomon (biblical character), 23–24, 55, 67, 73, 89, 157
Solovyev, Vladimir, 82